ANCIENT INDIA

ANCIENT INDIA

ITS
LANGUAGE AND RELIGIONS

H. OLDENBERG

GYAN

Published by

Gyan Publishing House
5, Ansari Road
Daryaganj, New Delhi-110002
Phone: 011-47034999, 9811692060
E-mail: books@gyanbooks.com

Distribution Network
gyanbooks.com
India, USA, Canada, UK, Australia, France

ISBN: 978-81-212-8981-8 (PB)
First Published, 1896

2nd Impression 2023

Printed at: Gyan Press, Delhi.

ANCIENT INDIA

AUTHOR: H. OLDENBERG

ANCIENT INDIA

ITS

LANGUAGE AND RELIGIONS

BY

PROF. H. OLDENBERG

CHICAGO
THE OPEN COURT PUBLISHING COMPANY
(LONDON: 17 JOHNSON'S COURT, FLEET ST., E. C.)
1896

TABLE OF CONTENTS.

THE STUDY OF SANSKRIT.

THE study of Sanskrit, the science of the antiquities of India, is about a century old. It was in the year 1784 that a number of men acting in Calcutta as judges or administrative officers of the East India Company, formed themselves into a scientific society, the Asiatic Society. We may say that the founding of the Asiatic Society was contemporaneous with the rise of a new branch of historical inquiry, the possibility of which preceding generations had barely or never thought of.

Englishmen began the work ; soon it was taken up by other nations; and in the course of time, in a much greater degree than is the case with the study of hieroglyphic and cuneiform inscriptions, it has become ever more distinctly a branch of inquiry peculiarly German.

The little band of workers who are busy in the workshops of this department of science, have not been accustomed to have the eyes of other men turned upon their doings—their successes and failures. But, in spite, nay, rather in consequence of this, it is right that an attempt should be made to invite even the most disinterested to an inspection of these places of industry, and to point out, piece by piece, the work, or at least part of the work, that has been done there.

There still lies formless in the workshops of this department of inquiry many a block of unhewn stone, which perhaps will forever resist the shaping hand. But still, under the active chisel, many a form has become visible, from whose features distant times and the past life of a strange people look down upon us—a people who are related to us, yet whose ways are so far removed in every respect from our ways.

We shall first cast a glance at the beginning of Indian research toward the close of the last century. We shall trace the way in which the new science, after the first hasty survey of its territory, at once concentrated its efforts to a more profound investigation of its subject and advanced to an incomparably broader plane of study. We shall, above all, follow the difficult course pursued in the study of the Veda, the most important of the literary remains of ancient India, a production with which even the works of the oldest Buddhism are not to be compared in point of historical importance. Of the problems that this science encountered, its aspirations, and of the successes that attended its efforts in solving difficult questions, we may venture to give a description, or at least an outline.

I.

The first effective impulse to the study of Sanskrit and Sanskrit literature was given by Sir William Jones, who, in 1783, embarked for India to assume the post of Judge of the Supreme Court of Judicature at Fort William. The honor of having inaugurated a new era of philological inquiry, was heightened by the lustre and charm of personal character which this gifted and versatile man exerted upon his contemporaries. In prose and in verse Jones is extolled by his friends of both sexes as the phœnix of his time, "the most enlightened of the sons of men"—encomiums many of which a calmer and more distant observer would be inclined to modify. The correspondence and other memoranda of Jones, which exist in great abundance,* furnish the reader of to-day rather the picture of an indefatigable and euphuistic *dilettante*, than that of an earnest investigator,—apart from the fact that he was alike greatly deficient in discernment and zeal.

As a young man we find Jones engaged in reading and reproducing in English verse, the works of Persian and Arabian poets; occasionally also with glimpses into Chinese literature. Then, again, a project of his own, an heroic epic—a sort of new Æneid, for which, and certainly with ingenuity enough, the Phœnician mythological deities were impressed into service—was to celebrate the perfections of the English constitution. On the journey to India this man of thirty-seven sketched a catalogue of the works, which, God granting him life, he hoped to write after celebrated models. These models were carefully designated opposite the separate projects of the outline. By the side of this heroic epic (after the pattern of Homer), we find a history of the war with America (after the patterns of Thucydides and Polybius), a philosophical and historical dialogue (after the pattern of Plato), and other plans of similar works.

With this feeling of omnipotent self-assurance, wholly untroubled with doubts, Jones was placed in India before the task of opening a way into the gigan-

*Edited by his biographer, Lord Teignmouth, and often given with more completeness than appears advisable considering the panegyrical character of the biography.

tic masses of an unknown literature, of a strange and beautiful poetry. He was as well qualified for the purpose (perhaps in a higher degree so) as many a more earnest and gifted scholar might have been.

The situation of affairs which he found in India forced it upon the European rulers of the land as a duty, to acquaint themselves with the Sanskrit language and its literature. The rapid extension and at the same time the redoubled activity of the English rule made it inconceivable that the existence of the old indigenous civilization and literature of the nation could long remain ignored or merely superficially recognized.

Preëminently did this necessity assert itself in the administration of justice, where the policy of the East India Company imperatively demanded that the natives should be suffered to retain as many of their laws and customs as it was possible to concede them. Already, in an act of parliament passed in 1772 in regard to the affairs of the company, a measure had been incorporated, at the suggestion of Warren Hastings, providing that Mohammedan and Indian lawyers should take part in court proceedings, in order to give effect to native lāws and assist in the formulation of judgments. The dependence that thus resulted, of European judges upon the reliability or unreliability of Indian pandits, must have been trying indeed, to the conscientious jurist; for the assertions of Indian councillors as to the principles of the Law of inheritance, contract, etc., contained in the native books, were subject to no control.

Warren Hastings, in order to obviate the difficulty, had a digest made by several Brahmanical jurisconsults from the old Sanskrit law books, and this was translated into English. The undertaking had but little success, principally because no European was to be found who could translate directly from the Sanskrit. A translation had first to be made from Sanskrit into Persian and from Persian again into English.* The necessity therefore of gaining direct access to the Sanskrit language was unquestionable. The undertaking was not an easy one, though it was still quite different from such apparently impossible feats of philological ingenuity as the deciphering of hieroglyphic and cuneiform inscriptions.

The knowledge and likewise the use of Sanskrit in India had lived on in unbroken tradition.† There were countless pandits who knew Sanskrit as well as the scholars of the Middle Ages knew Latin, and who were eminently competent to teach the language. It was easy to overcome the opposing Brahmanical prejudices. To become master, however, of the obstacles which emanated from the indescribably intricate and perverted grammatical system‡ of the Hindus, offered greater difficulties, which could only be overcome by patience and enthusiasm.

Just at the first moments of this trouble came the arrival of Sir William Jones in India. Immediately he was the central figure. From him came the founding of the Asiatic Society; from him, the impulse to a new revision of the Hindu law of contract and inheri-

* Published in 1776, under the title, "A Code of Gentoo Law."

† This is the case at the present time. Compare, upon this point, Max Müller's "India what can it teach us" p. 78 et seq.

‡ The original complaint of Paulinus a S. Bartholomaeo, a missionary in India about the time of Jones, is well known.—"The devil, with a phenomenal display of ingenuity and craft, had incited the Brahmanical sages to invent a language so rich and so complex, that its mysteries might be concealed not only from the people at large, but even from the very scholars who were conversant with it."

tance, this time undertaken on a surer basis. He assembled about him competent Brahmans versed in Sanskrit. In the year 1790 he wrote: "Every day I talk Sanskrit with the pandits; I hope before I leave India to understand it as I understand Latin."

It was not now a question of research, but of acquisition, of study; that clear and satisfactory results might rapidly be acquired, and that a proper selection of noteworthy productions of the Hindu mind might be made and presented before the eyes of all. Jones translated the most delightful of all Hindu dramas, the story of the touching fate of the ascetic maiden, Sakuntala, who in the sylvan quiet of her retreat was seen and loved by the kingly hunter Dushjanta—a work, full of the most delicate sentiment, exhaling fragrance like the summer splendor of Indian Nature, and sung in the delicate rhythms of Kalidasa, of inspired eloquence.*

Still more important than the version of Sakuntala was the publication of a second great work, which Jones translated, the *Laws of Manu.* It seemed as though a Lycurgus of a primitive oriental era had come to light; for this wonderful picture of a strange people's life was ascribed to the remotest antiquity—a description of Brahmanical rule by the grace of Brahma, magnified and distorted by priestly pride, in which the people are nothing, the prince is little, the priest is everything. In the face of such an abruptly accumulated mass of unexpected revelations, respecting an an-

* It was formerly thought, for reasons that have not withstood the assault of criticism, that Kalidasa flourished in the first century before Christ; it was the custom to compare him to the Roman poets of the Augustan era, whose contemporaries he in that event would about have been. In point of fact he must be assigned to an era several centuries later,—about the sixth century after Christ.

cient civilization hitherto removed from all knowledge, how could one resist an attempt to give to that civilization and its language a place among known civilizations and languages? Wherever the eye turned weighty and pregnant suggestions offered themselves, and with them the temptation to let fancy stray in aimless sallies. What is more, Jones was in no wise the man to resist such a temptation. The vocabulary and the grammatical structure of Sanskrit convinced him that the ancient language of the Hindus was related to those of the Greeks, Romans, and Germans, that it must have been derived with them from a common mother tongue.* But side by side with the conception of this incomparably suggestive idea, innumerable fanciful theories abound in the works of Jones, concerning the relationship of the primitive peoples, where everything was found to be in some way related to everything else. Now the Hindu tongue was identified with that of the Old Testament; now Hindu civilization was brought into connection with South American civilization. Buddha was said to be Woden; and the pyramids and sphinxes of Egypt were claimed to show the style of the same workmen who built the Hindu cave-temples and chiseled the ancient images of Buddha.

Fortunately for the new study of Sanskrit, the continuation of the work begun by Jones fell to one of the most cautious and comprehensive observers of facts that have ever devoted their attention and talent to

*The identity of Hindu words with those of Latin, Greek, and other languages had been noticed by several before Jones, and likewise the correct explanation of this phenomenon, namely the kinship of the Hindu nation with the Latins and Greeks, had been declared by Father Pons as early as 1740. For fuller account, see Benfey, "History of the Science of Language," (*Geschichte der Sprachwissenschaft*) pp. 222, 333–341.

the study of oriental literatures. This was Henry Thomas Colebrooke (born 1765; went to India 1782), the most active in the active band of Indian administrative officers. He officiated now as an officer of the government, now again as a justice, then as diplomatist—a man well versed in Indian agriculture and Indian trade. One can scarcely regard without astonishment the multitude of disclosures which, during the long period he devoted to Sanskrit, he was able to make from his incomparable collection of manuscripts. These to-day are among the principle treasures of the India Office Library. From the province of Indian poetry, Colebrooke, who well knew the limits of his own power, kept aloof. But in the literature of law, grammar, philosophy, and astronomy, he had a wide reading, which in scope may never again be reached. He it was who made the first comprehensive disclosure in regard to the literature of the Veda.

Colebrooke's investigations are poor in hypotheses; we may say he withheld too much from seeking to comprehend the historical genesis of the subjects with which he dealt. But he established the actual foundation of broad provinces of Hindu research; filled with wonder himself at the ever widening vistas of that literature which were now revealed to him, and awakening our just wonder by the sure and patient toil with which he sought to penetrate into those distant parts.

While Colebrooke was at the height of his activity, interest in Hindu inquiry began to be awakened in a country which has done more than any other land to make of Hindu research a firm and well-established science—in Germany.

For the discoveries of Jones and Colebrooke there

could have been no more receptive soil than the Germany of that time, full of spirited interest in the old national poetry of all nations and occupied with the stirring movements rife in its own philosophy and literature. Apparently, indeed, the latter were closely allied to the spirit of the distant Hindu literature; for here too oriental romanticism and poetical thought sought no less boldly than the absolute philosophy of Germany, to penetrate to the primal and formless source of all forms. From the beginning, poets stood in the foremost ranks among the Sanskritists of Germany; there were the two Schlegels and Friedrich Rückert, and beside these, careful and unassuming, the great founder of grammatical science, Franz Bopp.

In the year 1808 appeared Friedrich Schlegel's work, *Ueber die Sprache und Weisheit der Inder* (The Language and Learning of the Hindus). From what was known to him of Hindu poetry and speculation, and according to his own ideas of the laws and aims of the human mind, Schlegel, with warm and fanciful eloquence, drew a picture of India as a land of exalted primitive wisdom. Hindu religion and Hindu poetry he described as replete with exuberant power and light, in comparison with which even the noblest philosophy and poetry of Greece was but a feeble spark The time from which the masterpieces of the Hindus dated, appeared to him a distant, gigantic, primeval age of spiritual culture. There was the home of those earnest teachings, full of gloomy tragedy, of the soul's migration, and of the dark fate which ordains for all beings their ways and their end:

> Obedient to this purpose set, they wander; from God to plants;
> Here, in the abhorred world of existence, that ever moves to destruction.

While Schlegel gave to the world this fanciful

picture of Hindu wisdom, highly effective from its prophetic perspectives, but still wanting in sober truth, Bopp applied himself, more unassumingly, but with an incomparably deeper grasp and patient sagacity, to investigating the grammatical structure of Sanskrit; and, on the recognized fact of the relationship of this language with the Persian and the principal European tongues, to establishing the science of comparative grammar. In the year 1816 appeared his *Conjugationssystem der Sanskritsprache in Vergleichung mit jenem der griechischen, lateinischen, persischen, und germanischen Sprache* (Conjugational System of the Sanskrit Language in Comparison with that of the Greek, Latin, Persian, and Teutonic Languages).

This was no longer merely an attempt to find isolated similarities in the sounds of the words of related languages, but an attempt to trace back not only uniformities but also differences to their fixed laws; and thus in the life and growth of these languages, as they sprang from a common root and evolved themselves into a rich complexity, to discover more and more the traces of a necessity dominated by definite principles.

We can here only briefly touch upon the investigations made during the last seventy years, for which Bopp laid the foundation by the publication of his work. Rarely have such astonishing results been achieved by science as here. Elucidative of the early history of the languages of Homer and the old Italian monuments before they acquired the form in which we now find them written, the most unexpected witnesses were brought to give testimony; namely, the languages of the Hindus, the Germans, the Slavs, and the Celts. Of these related tongues, the one sheds light upon the obscure features of the others, just as natural history explains the stunted organs of some animals by pointing out the same organs in their original, perfect form, in other animals.

The picture of the mother tongue, whose filial descendants are the languages of our linguistic family, was no longer seen in merely vague or doubtful features. The laws under whose dominion the system of sounds and forms in the separate derived languages have been developed from the mother tongue, are being ascertained ever more fully and formulated ever more sharply.

From the very beginning the essential instrument, yes, the very foundation of this investigation, was the Sanskrit language. In the beginning, faith in the primitiveness of Sanskrit in comparison with the related languages was too strong. During the last few years, however, this erroneous conception has been fully rectified; and this in itself is a decided step in advance. We know now that the apparently simpler and clearer state of Sanskrit in sounds and forms is in many respects less primitive than the complicated relations of other languages, *e. g.*, the Greek; and that we must often set out from these languages rather than from the Sanskrit, in order to make possible the explanation of Sanskrit forms. Thus Sanskrit now receives back the light which it has furnished for the historical understanding of the European languages.*

* It may be permissible here to illustrate this reversion of methods in a single point that has become of especially great importance to grammar. The Greek has five short vowels, *a, e, o, i, u*. The Sanskrit has *i* and *u* corresponding to *i* and *u*; but to the three sounds, *a, e, o* corresponds in Sanskrit only a single vowel *a*. Thus, for example, the Greek *apo* (English, *from*) reads in Sanskrit *apa;* the *a* of the first syllable, and the *o* of the second syllable of the

I must not attempt to follow in detail the course which the science of comparative grammar, apart from its connection with Hindu research, has taken. While the two branches of the study were rapidly advanced by Germans particularly, and likewise in France by the sagacious Burnouf, new material kept pouring in from India no less rapidly. In two countries on the outskirts of Indian civilization, in the Himalayan valleys of Nepal, and in Ceylon, the sacred literature of the Buddhists, which had disappeared in India proper, was brought to light in two collections, one in Sanskrit and one in the popular dialect Pali. The ingenuity of Prinseps succeeded in deciphering the oldest Indian written characters on inscriptions and coins. In Calcutta was undertaken and completed in the Thirties the publication of the *Mahabharata*, a gigantic heroic poem of almost a hundred thousand

Greek word is thus represented in Sanskrit by *a*. Or, to use another example, the Greek *menos* (English, *courage*) is in Sanskrit *manas;* Greek *epheron* (I carried)—*abharam*. What now is the original, *i. e.*, what existed in the Indo-Germanic mother tongue for the three sounds of the Greek *a*, *e*, *o*, or the single sound of the Sanskrit *a*? When scholars began to study comparative philology upon the basis of the Sanskrit they thought the *a*—and this was a conclusion apparently supported by the simplicity of the language—to be alone the original sound; and were led to believe that this vowel was later divided on European soil into three sounds, *a*, *e*, *o*. Investigations of the most recent time—and for these we are to thank Amelung, Burgman, John Schmidt, and others—have shown that the development of the vowel system took the opposite course. The vowels *a*, *e*, *o* were already in the Indo-Germanic mother tongue; and in Sanskrit, or more accurately, before the time of Sanskrit, in the language which the ancestors of the Indians and Persians spoke when both formed *one* people, these vowels were merged into a single vowel Thus the *e* of *esti* and the *o* of *apo* are more original than the *a* of *asti*, *apa*.

Now, we find in Sanskrit that where the Greek *e* corresponds to the Sanskrit *a*, certain consonants preceding this vowel, as. *e.g.*, *k*, are affected in a different way by the latter, than in instances where for the *a* of Sanskrit the Greek *a* or *o* is used. From the linguistic form of Sanskrit alone, which in the one case as in the other has *a*, it would not be intelligible why the *k* should each time meet a different fate. The Greek, in that it has preserved the original differences of the vowels, gives the key to an understanding of the peculiar transformations which have taken place in the *k*-sound in large and important groups of Sanskrit words.

couplets, in whose vast cantos with their labyrinth of episodes and sub-episodes many generations of poets have brought together legends of the heroes and days of the olden time, of their struggles and flagellations.

The sum and substance of all this newly-acquired knowledge has been incorporated in the great work of a Norwegian, who became, in Germany, a German—in the *Indische Alterthumskunde* (Hindu Antiquities) of Christian Lassen.

Lassen did not belong to the great pioneers of science, like Bopp. It must also be said that often that sagacity of philological thought is wanting in him, which sheds light on questions even where it affords no definite solution of them. And, indeed, was it not a herculean undertaking, a work like that of the Danaides, to explore the older periods of the Hindu past when, as the chief sources of information, one was solely limited to the great epic, and the law book of Manu? Even a surer critical power than Lassen possessed could not have discovered much of history in the nebulous confusion of legends, in the invented series of kings in *Mahabharata*, and in that colorless uniformity which the style of the Hindu Virgils spreads unchangeably over the enormous periods of time of which they assume to inform us. In spite of this, Lassen's *Antiquities*—the work of tireless diligence and rare learning—stands as a landmark in the history of Hindu investigations, uniting all the results of past time, and pointing out anew, by the very things in which it is lacking, still untried undertakings.

Just at this time, however, when the first volume of Lassen's work, treating of the earliest periods, appeared, came the beginning of a movement which has severed the development of Hindu studies into two parts. New personalities appeared upon the scene and pushed to the front a new series of problems, for the solution of which an apparently inexhaustible, and to this day, in a certain sense, a still inexhaustible supply of freshly acquired material was offered. This was the most important acquisition that has ever been added to our knowledge of the world's literature through any one branch of oriental inquiry—the acquisition of the *Veda* for science.

II.

CONSIDERING the circumstances, this acquisition of the Veda for science can hardly be accounted a discovery. The existence and position in Hindu literature of this great work, had long been known. At every step the writings that had previously been brought to light, pointed to the Veda as the source from which all proceeded—even more strikingly than in the literature of Greece, we are led back, at every turn, to the poems of Homer. Manuscripts of the Vedic texts, moreover, were to be found, not only in India; they had long been possessed in great numbers by the libraries of Europe. But an attempt had scarcely, if at all, been made to lay hold of these and see if in the unmeasurable chaos of this mass of writings a firm ground for science could not be acquired.

The Sanskrit of the great epic poems, or of Kalidasa, was understood well enough; but of the dialect in which the most important parts of the Veda were written, no more was known than one familiar with the French of to-day would know of the language of the Troubadours. Without going deeply into the study it was easy to discern its inherent difficulties from the unwonted singularity of the text and its strange contents, which, in part at least, were extremely complicated, and often involved in a maze of minor details. Would an earnest explorer of this territory, even in case he succeeded, be rewarded for his pains?

It was a band of young German scholars who bent their energies to this work. Most of them are, or were till very lately, among us—Max Müller, Roth, and Weber. Two others, whose names should not be omitted here, Adalbert Kuhn and Benfey, died some years ago. There was no need of undertaking great expeditions, such as were those that set out for the investigation of Egyptian and Babylonian antiquity. Those monuments in whose colossal and strange forms fragments of a primeval age meet the eye, were wanting in India. The knowledge which was to be acquired was not contained in inscriptions, but in manuscripts.* Our scholars repaired to London for a greater or less length of time, and the work was begun among the store of manuscripts possessed by the East India House.

There was no lack of confidence. "It would be a disgrace," wrote Roth, "to the criticism and the ingenuity of our century which has deciphered the stone inscriptions of the Persian kings and the books of Zoroaster, if it did not succeed in reading in this enormous literature the intellectual history of the Hindu nation."

Much that Roth expected has been accomplished or is on the way towards accomplishment. Of much that was hoped for at that time, we can now say that it was unattainable, and understand why. What has

* The royal library at Berlin also acquired and owns a rich collection of Sanskrit manuscripts, for which a foundation was laid by the purchase, at the command of Frederick William IV., of the Chambers' manuscripts.

been attained, however, has given to the picture, which science formed of Hindu antiquity, an entirely different aspect. Unbounded in extent, this picture formerly seemed to lose itself in the nebulous depths of an immeasurable past. Now, determinate limits have been found, and the remotest initial point has been discovered for verifiable history. Authentic sources were disclosed, leading to the earliest age of Hindu civilization, from which, and regarding which, historical testimony in the usual sense of the word became accessible; and instead of the twilight, peopled with uncertain, shadowy giants, in which the epic poems made those times appear, the Veda opened to us a reality which we may hope to understand. Or, if in many instances, instead of the hoped for forms, it has afforded the eye but an empty space, even this was a step in advance. For then it was at least shown that the knowledge which was sought was not to be had; and that which had been given as such, had disclosed itself as an imaginative picture born of the caprice of a later legend-maker.

The literature of epic poetry, apparently, could no longer lay claim to an incalculable antiquity; it sank back into a sort of Middle Ages, behind which the newly discovered, real antiquity loomed forth, studding the horizon of historical knowledge with significant forms. We shall now see how the task of understanding the Veda was accomplished, and shall describe at the same time what it was that had thus been acquired. We have here a newly disclosed literature of venerable antiquity, rich in marks of earnest effort, logically developed in sharply, nay rigidly, characterized forms; we have a newly discovered piece of history, forming the historical—or shall we say unhistorical?—beginnings of a people related to us by race, who at an early day set out in paths distinctly removed from the ways of all other peoples, and created their own strange forms of existence, bearing in them the germs of the misfortunes they have suffered.

By what means did we succeed in understanding the Veda?

Almost all the more important parts of the Vedic literature—for the Veda, like the Bible, is not a separate text, but a literature with wide ramifications—are preserved in numerous, and, for the most part, relatively modern manuscripts. Only rarely are they older than a few centuries; since in the destructive climate of India it could not be otherwise. The texts, however, of these later manuscripts descend from remote antiquity.

Before they came to be written in *the present* manuscripts, or written in manuscript-form at all, they encountered, in the course of great periods of time, many and manifold misfortunes. It is the task of the philological inquirer to ascertain the character of these events—to determine the genetic history of the texts. It may be said that these texts in the shape they have been transmitted to us, resemble paintings by old masters, which bear unmistakable traces of alternate injuries and attempted restorations by competent and incompetent hands. What we want to know, so far as it lies in our power, is the form and general character in which they originally existed.

The period to which the origin of the old Vedic poems belongs, we cannot assign in years, nor yet in centuries. But we know that these poems existed, when there was not a city in India, but only hamlets and castles; when the names of the powerful tribes which at a later time assumed the first rank among the nations of India were not even mentioned, no more so than in the Germany which Tacitus described were mentioned the names of Franks and Bavarians. It was the period of migrations, of endless, turbulent feuds among small unsettled tribes with their nobles and priests; people fought for pastures, and cows, and arable land. It was the period of conflict between the fair-skinned immigrants, who called themselves Arya, and the natives, the "dark people," the "unbelievers that propitate not the Gods."

As yet the thought and belief of the Hindus did not seek the divine in those formless depths in which later ages conceived the idea of the eternal and hidden Brahma. Wherever in nature the brightest pictures met the eye and the mightiest tones struck the ear, there were their Gods—the luminous arch of heaven, the red hues of dawn, the thundering storm-god and his followers, the winds. The Vedic Aryans had not yet reached their later abode on the two powerful sister streams, the Ganges and the Yumna; the Sindhu (Indus) was still for them the "Mother Stream," of which one of the oldest poets of the Rig Veda says: *

> "From earth along the reach of Heaven riseth the sound;
> Ceaseless the roar of her waters, the bright one.
> As floods of thundering rain, poured from the darkened cloud-bosom,
> So rushes the Sindu, like the steer, the bellowing one."

The poetry of the Rig Veda dates from the time of those wanderings and struggles that took place on the Indus and its tributary streams. Certain families exercised the functions of priestly offices, and

* Hundreds of Vedic melodies have been handed down to us in a form the interpretation of which can be subject to no real doubt. As it appears, they are the oldest but unfortunately the poorest memorials of musical antiquity.

possessed the acquisitions of an artificially connected speech together with a simple form of chant using but few tones. These families created Vedic poetry, and transmitted the art to their posterity. The songs of the Rig Veda, which are almost all sacrificial songs, were not really what we call popular poetry. We do not hear in them the language that pours forth from the soul of a nation, as it communes in poetical rhythm with itself. It was a poetry that wanted mainly the proper hearers—the masses of the people who spoke through the mouth of the poet. Their hearers were God Agni, God Indra, or Goddess Dawn; and the poet was not he whom the passionate impulses of his own soul or his own love of song and legend impelled to sing, but he was mainly one who belonged to a poet-family—one of the families of men who in the course of time became united as a caste and erected ever more insuperable barriers between their sacred existence and the profane reality of daily life. For the gods such a poet only "could frame a worthy poem, as an experienced, skillful wheelwright makes a wagon,"—a poem which would be rewarded by the rich princely lords of the sacrifice, with steeds and kine, with golden ornaments and female slaves from the spoils of war. "Thy blessing," says a Vedic poet to a God,*

> "Rests with the givers,
> With the victors, the many valiant heroes,
> Who make gifts to us of clothing, kine, and horses;
> May they rejoice in the splendor and plenty of divine bounty.
>
> Let all things waste that they have won
> Who, without rewarding, would profit by our hymns to heaven.
> The godless ones, that boast their fortune,
> The transgressors—cast them from the light of day."

It has been fatal for all thought and poetry in India, that a second world, filled with strangely fantastic

* Rig Veda V. 42, 8–9.

shapes, was established at an early day beside the real world. This was the place of sacrifice with its three sacred fires and the schools in which the virtuosos of the sacrificial art were educated—a sphere of strangest activity and the playground of a subtle, empty mummery, whose enervating power over the spirit of an entire nation we can scarcely comprehend in its full extent. The poetry of the Rig Veda shows us this process of disease at an early stage; but it is there, and much of that which constitutes the essence of the Rig Veda, is rooted in it.

In the foreground stands the sacrifice, and throughout, only the sacrifice. "By sacrifice the Gods made sacrifice; these regulations were the first," it is said in a verse which is thrice repeated in the Rig Veda. The praise of the God for whom the sacrificial offerings were intended, his power, his victories, and the prayers for possessions which were hoped for in return for human offerings—the prosperity of flocks and posterity, long life, destruction of enemies, the hated and the godless—such is the subject-matter of the multitudinous repetitions that recur throughout the hymns of the Rig Veda. Still, among these verse-making sacrificers there was not an utter absence of real poets. And thus among the stereotyped implorations and songs of praise we find here and there a great and beautiful picture—the wonder of the poet's soul at the bright marvels of nature or the deep expression of an earnest inner life. A poet from the priestly family of the Bharadvajas sings of the goddess Ushas, the dawn: *

* The Indian word Ushas is related to the Greek Eos, the Latin Aurora.

"We see thee, thou lovely one; far, far, thou shinest.
To heaven's heights thy brilliant light-beams dart.
In beauteous splendor shimmering, unveilest thou thy bosom,
Radiant with heaven's sheen, celestial queen of dawn!

"The red bulls draw their chariot,
Where in thy splendor thou o'erspread'st the heavens;
Thou drivest away night; as a hero, a bow-man,
As a swift charioteer frighteneth his enemies.

"A beautiful path has been made for thee in the mountain.
Thou unconquerable one, thou risest from out the waters.
So bring thou us treasures to revive us on
Our further course, queenly daughter of heaven."*

Another poet sings of Parjanya, the rain God: †

"Like the driver who forward whips his steeds,
So he urges onward his messengers, the clouds.
From afar the thunder-tone of the lion arises
When the God makes rain pour from the clouds.

"Parjanya's lightnings dart, the winds blow;
The floods pour from heaven; up spring grass and plants.
To all that lives and moves a quickening is imparted,
When the God scatters his seeds on the earth.

"At his command the earth bows deeply down;
At his command hoofed creatures come to life;
At his command bloom forth the bright flowers:
May Parjanya grant us strong defence!

"A flood of rain hast thou sent; now cease;
Thou didst make penetrable the desert wastes.
For us thou hast caused plants to grow for food,
And the prayer of men thou hast fulfilled."

But we must turn from the description of Vedic poetry to examine the fortune that this production encountered on its way from distant antiquity to the present time, from the sacrificial places on the Indus to the workshops of the English and German philologists. Here a conspicious fact is to be dwelt upon,

* Rig Veda VI. 64. The hymn following is V. 83.

† This God also reappears among the kindred peoples of Europe, as Fiörgynn in the northern mythology, and among the Lithuanians and Prussians as the God Perkunas, of whom an old chronicle says: "Perkunas was the third idol; and him the people besought for storms, so that during his time they had rain and fair weather and suffered not from the thunder and the lightning."

which belongs to the strangest phenomena of Indian history, so rich in strange events. The hymns of the Rig Veda, as well as the hymns of the other Vedas, have been composed, collected, and transmitted to succeeding ages. There has been incorporated in them a very large sacerdotal prose literature, developed throughout the older and later divisions, and treating of the art and symbolism of sacrifice. There have also arisen heretical sects, like the Buddhists, who denied the authority of the Veda, and instead of its teachings reverenced as a sacred text the code of ordinances proclaimed by Buddha. *And all this has taken place without the art of writing.*

In the Vedic ages writing was not known. At the time when Buddhism arose it was indeed known—the Indians probably learned to write from Semites—but it was used only for inditing short communications in practical life, not for writing books. We have very sure and characteristic information as to the rôle which the art of writing played, or rather did not play, in the church life of the Buddhists at a comparatively late age, say about 400 B. C. The sacred text of this sect affords a picture, executed even in its minutest features, of life in the houses and parks which the brethren inhabited. We can see the Buddhist monks pursue their daily life from morning to night; we can see them in their wanderings and during their rest, in solitude and in intercourse with other monks, or laymen; we know the equipment of the places occupied by them, their furniture, and the contents of their store-rooms. But nowhere do we hear that they read their sacred texts or copied them; nowhere, that in the dwellings of the monks such things as writing utensils or manuscripts were found.

The memory of the spiritual brethren, "rich in hearing,"—what we to-day call a well-read man was then called one rich in hearing,—took the place of a cloister library; and if the knowledge of some indispensable text,—as, *e. g.*, the formula of confession which had to be recited at the full and new moon in the assembly of the brethren,—was in danger of being lost among a body of priests, they acted on the dictum laid down in an old Buddhistic ordinance: "By these monks a monk shall immediately be sent to a neighboring parish. He must be thus instructed: 'Go, Brother, and when thou hast learned by heart the formula of confession, the complete one or the abreviated one, come back to us.'"

It must be admitted that under such circumstances all the conditions for the existence of books, and the relations between books and reader—if it be allowed me for the sake of brevity to use these expressions—must have been of a very different nature than in an age of writing or one of printing. A book could then exist only on condition that a body of men existed among whom it was taught and learned and transmitted from generation to generation. A book could be known only at the price of learning it by heart, or of having some one at hand who had thus learned it. Texts of a content which only claimed a passing notice, could not as a rule exist. This was fatal for historical writing and generally speaking for all profane literature. Above all, the existing texts were subjected to the disfigurements that errors of memory, carelessness, or attempts at improvement on the part of the transmitters must have imported into them.

Under conditions such as have been described above, the poetry of the Rig Veda has been handed down from generation to generation through many centuries. Separate poems were brought into the collection in the course of oral compilation and transmission. The collection was re-corrected on repeated occasions and was brought to greater completeness; again only by oral compilation and transmission. It is conceivable enough that thus the original structure yes, even the existence itself of special hymns was often injured, effaced, or destroyed. Remodeling destroyed their form. The lines of division between hymns standing side by side would often be forgotten and numbers of them would be merged into an apparent unity. Modern, and easily intelligible terms drove out the obsolete phrases and the ancient word-forms—often the most valuable remains for the investigator, whom they help to explain the history of the language, just as the scientist deduces from fossil remains the history of organic life.

Especially fatal was it for the old and true form of the Vedic hymns that they have been stretched upon the Procrustean bed of grammatical analysis. Earlier and more strongly than in any other nation of antiquity, was interest and pleasure taken in India in scientifically dissecting language. Closely examining the separate sounds of speech and their underlying modifications, they employed exceptional ingenuity and discrimination in constructing a system from which, when it became known in Europe, the science of our century found ample reason to learn much that was marvellous. The ingenuity and penetration of the students of Vedic literature has been burdened like a curse with that genuinely Hindu trait, subtlety; the joy—which at times seems to border on maliciousness—of stretching and forcing things into an artistic garment, of building up labyrinths of fine points, in whose involved courses the skilled and cunning student ostentatiously thought himself able to find his way. Thus, in this grammatical science, understanding and misunderstanding of the real truth are mingled in inexplicable confusion. That under the hands of such linguistic theorists the precious wealth of the old Vedic hymns has not remained inviolate, is easily comprehended. In some cases, isolated details of the traditions of prior epochs were caught and clung to with felicitous acumen ; in others, no hesitation was had in wiping out of existence entire domains of old and genuine phenomena to suit half-correct theories, so that the most patient ingenuity of modern science will only be able to restore in part what has been lost.

Finally, however, the caprice under which the hymns of the old singers must have suffered, had its end. The more people accustomed themselves to see in these poems not merely beautiful and efficacious prayers but a sacred revelation of the divine, the higher did their transmitted form—even when this is, or seems to be, of necessity, so irregular—rise in the respect of theologians, and the more careful must they have been to describe and preserve this form with all its dissimilarities.

We possess a remarkable work—it is composed in verse like many Hindu treatises and hand-books—in which a grammarian, Çaunaka, who must probably be placed about the time 400 B. C., has given a deep and unusually well-planned survey of the vocal peculiarities of the Rig Veda text. The study of Çaunaka's work affords us the proof that *from that time on* the Vedic hymns, protected by the united care of grammatical and religious respect for letters, have suffered no further appreciable corruptions. The most important manuscripts of the Rig Veda which we know, may be two thousand years later than this hand-book of Çaunaka's, but they bear all tests in a remarkable way if we compare them with it.

The Rig Veda, indeed, which that Hindu scholar found, was not unlike a ruin. And it was hardly possible by the help of Hindu scholarship to transmit it to posterity in a better condition than it was received But still the conscientious diligence of the Hindu linguists and divines accomplished something: for the last two thousand years it has preserved these venerable fragments from the dangers of further decay. They lie there, untouched, just as they were in the days of Çaunaka. And the investigation of our day, which has already succeeded in bringing forth from many a field of ruins the living features of a by-gone existence, is at work among them, now with the bold grasp of confident divination, now in the quiet uniformity of slowly advancing deliberation, to deduce whatever it may of the real forms of those old priestly poems.

III.

We may say, that the greatest undertakings planned and the most important results achieved in the field of Sanskrit research, are linked with the names of German investigators. If we add that this could not easily be otherwise, it is not from national vanity; we should but express the actual facts of the case, based upon the development of the science. It was natural that the first movements toward the founding of Hindu research, the first attempts to grasp the vastly accumulated material and find provisional forms for it, should have been the work of Englishmen, men who spent a good part of their lives in India, and were there brought in constant contact with native Sanskrit scholars. But not less natural was it that the honor of instituting further progress and gaining a deeper insight should be accorded to Germans. The two fields of knowledge by which, especially, life and power were imparted to Hindu investigations were and are essentially German. These are comparative grammar, which we may say was founded by Bopp, and that profound and potent science, or perhaps more correctly expressed art, of philology, which was practiced by Gottfried Hermann, and likewise by Karl Lachmann, a man imbued with the proud spirit of Lessing, full of acute and purposeful ability, exact and truthful in small matters as in great. Representatives of this philology, moved to antipathy by many characteristic features of the Hindu spirit, and not the least influenced by the assertion that Latin and Greek grammar has this or that to learn from the Sanskrit, might meet the new science of India with reserve or more than reserve. Still this could in no wise alter the truth that the study of Hindu texts, the investigation of Hindu literary remains, could be learned from no better teachers than from those masters who had succeeded in improving and interpreting the classical texts with unerring certainty and excellence of method.

It was a Leipsic disciple of Hermann and Haupt who, at the instigation of Burnouf, in 1845, in Paris, conceived the plan of publishing the Rig Veda with the commentary of its Hindu expounder, the abbot Sayana, who flourished in the 14th century after Christ. This was the great work of Max Müller, the first of of those fundamental undertakings on which Vedic philology rests. It was necessary above all to know how the Brahmins themselves translated the hymns of their forefathers, which were preserved in the Rig Veda, from the Vedic language into current Sanskrit, and how they solved the problems which the grammar of the Veda presented, by the means their own grammatical system offers. Herein lay the indispensable foundation of all further investigation. It was necessary to weigh the Hindu *traditions* concerning the explanation of the Veda, which erred in underestimation as well as overestimation, and to test the consequences of both errors, in order finally to learn the art of scientifically estimating them. This constitutes the great importance of Max Müller's work extending through a quarter of a century (1849–1874). To complete was easy, but to begin was exceedingly difficult; for most of the grammatical and theological texts which formed the basis for Sayana's deductions, were, when Max Müller began the work, books sealed with seven seals.

A few years after the first volume of Max Müller's Rig Veda appeared, two other scholars united in a work of still greater magnitude. It has long since become to all Sanskritists the most indispensable tool for their labors. I refer to the Sanskrit dictionary, compiled under the commission of the Academy of St. Petersburg, Russia, by Roth and Böhtlingk. It was intended to make a dictionary for a language the greatest and most important part of whose texts were still not in print. The work was similar to that which the Grimm Brothers began at the same time for the German language. Roth undertook the Vedic literature, the foundation of the whole; Böhtlingk the later periods. Friendly investigators, and especially Weber, helped them by bringing into use the known and accessible texts or manuscripts that were serviceable to them. The most important thing was, that the Veda had now for the first time—setting aside a few previous studies—to be gone through with a view to lexicography. The explanations which the Hindus themselves were wont to give of the words of the Vedic language were regarded as a valuable aid for understanding it. But the matter did not rest here. "We do not hold it," said the two compilers in their preface, "to be our task to acquire that understanding of the Veda which was current in India some centuries ago; but we seek the sense which the poets themselves gave to their hymns and maxims." They undertook "to get at the sense from the texts themselves, by collating all the passages related in word or meaning." In this way they hoped to re-establish the meaning of each word, not as a colorless conception, but in its individuality and therefore in its strength and beauty. The Veda was thus to re-acquire its living sense, the full wealth of its expression. The thought of the earliest antiquity was to appear to us in new forms full of life and reality.

The execution of this work, carried on with tenacious industry and brilliant success for four and twenty years (1852–1875), did not fall short of the magnitude of the plan originally conceived. In minor points we find it easy to point out numerous deficiencies and errors. The two compilers well knew that without that spirit of boldness which does not stand in fear of unavoidable errors, it were better never to undertake their task. In face, however, of the great value of that which they have accomplished, all faults sink into insignificance.

What a chasm separates their work from that of their predecessor, Wilson! * In Wilson's work there is little more than a fair enumeration of the meanings which Hindu traditions assigned to the words; for his dictionary the Veda scarcely exists, if it does so at all. Here in the work of Roth and Böhtlingk on the other hand, is brought to light the immense wealth, replete with oriental splendor, of the richest of all languages; the history of each word, and likewise the fortunes that have befallen it in the different periods of the literature and have determined its meaning, are brought before our eyes. The difference between the two great periods in which the development of Hindu research falls, could not be incorporated more clearly than in these two dictionaries. In the one instance are found the beginnings, which English science, resting immediately on the shoulders of the Indian pandits, has made; in the other is the continuation of English work conducted by strict philological methods to a breadth and depth incomparably beyond those beginnings, and at the head of this undertaking stand German scholars.

To Müller's great edition of the Rig Veda and to the St. Petersburg Dictionary further investigations have been added in great abundance, and these have more and more extended the limits of our knowledge of the Veda. Already a new generation of laborers have taken their places beside the original pioneers in these once so impassable regions. As a whole, or in its separate parts, the Rig Veda has been repeatedly

* Wilson's dictionary appeared in 1819; a second edition in 1832.

translated. Its stock of words and inflections has been studied and overhauled from ever new points of view and with ever new questions in mind. To many a picturesque word of the strong, harsh Vedic language its full weight has thus been given back.

The principles and practices according to which the old collectors and revisers of the Veda text proceeded, are now being examined by us with a view to being able to determine what came into their hands as tradition and what they themselves imported into the traditions. The readings of the passages quoted from the Rig Veda in the other Vedas are being collected, in order to trace in them the remains of the genuine and oldest textual form. The religion and mythology of the Veda have been described; the national life of the Vedic tribes has been portrayed in all its phases. The texts afford the data for such a portraiture of these features that it has justly been said that the description given surpasses in clearness and accuracy Tacitus's account of the national life of the Germans.* Finally an attempt has been made—or rather an attempt will have to be made, for even at this time the work is in its beginnings—to discover amid the masses of Vedic prayers and sacrificial hymns something which must be an especially welcome find to scientific curiosity—the beginning of the Indian Epic.†

There could be no doubt that in so poetical a period the pleasure of romancing produced abundant fruit. Short narratives, short hymns must then have

* H. Zimmer: *Altindisches Leben : die Cultur der vedischen Arier.* (Ancient Indian Life: the Civilization of the Vedic Aryans.) Berlin, 1879, p. vii.

† The remarks here made on the beginnings of the Indian Epic rest on conceptions which I have before briefly sought to establish. *Zeitschrift der Deutschen Morgenländ. Gesellsch.*, 1885, p. 52, et seq.

existed, enclosed, as it were, in narrow frames. Thus, in general, are the beginnings of epic poetry shaped, before poetic ability rises and ventures to narrate in wider scope and with more complicated structure the fate of men and heroes. It seemed, however, as though those beginnings of the Indian epic were lost. But they were preserved, though to be sure in a peculiarly fragmentary form. In the Rig Veda there is many a medley of apparently disconnected verses in which we have thought to discover the accumulated sweepings of poetic workshops. In fact we have here the fragmentary remains of epic narratives. These verses were once inserted in a prose framework; the narrative part of the Epic being in prose, and the speeches and counter-speeches in verse, just as, often, in Grimm's fairy-tales when the poor daughter of the king or the powerful dwarf has to speak an especially weighty or touching word, a rhyme or two appears.

Now, only the verses were memorized in their fixed original form by the Vedic tale-tellers. The prose, each new narrator would render with fresh words; until finally its original subject-matter fell into almost total oblivion, and the verses alone survived, appearing sometimes as a series of dialogues sufficiently long and full of meaning to enable us to gain an understanding of the whole, and then again as unrecognizable fragments no more admitting an inference as to their proper place and connection in the story of which they form a part than—to keep the same comparison—a couple of rhymes in one of Grimm's fairy-tales would enable us to restore the whole tale.

It may be permitted for the sake of making clear what has been said, to cite here a passage from one of those old narratives whose connection, at least as a whole, may be conjecturally determined.* The scene is between gods and demons, its subject is the great battle which was fought in heaven, the thunder fight, which for the strife-loving spirit of that age was the pattern of their own victories. Vritra, the envious fiend, kept the waters of the clouds in captivity, that they might not pour down upon the earth; but God Indra smote the demon with his thunderbolt and let the liberated waters flow. Indra—this must have been said in the lost prose introduction to the narrative—felt, as he entered the battle, too weak for his terrible opponent. The gods, faint-hearted, withdrew from his side. Only one offered himself as an ally, Vâyu (the wind),† the swiftest of the gods, but he demanded as a reward for his fidelity, part of the sacrificial draught of Soma, which men offer to Indra. Vâyu speaks:

> "Tis I. I come to thee the foremost, as is meet;
> Behind me march in full array, the Gods.
> Givest thou me, O Indra, but a share of sacrifice,
> And thou shalt do, with my alliance, valiant deeds of might."

Indra accepted the alliance:

> "Of the honied draught I give thee the first portion;
> Thine shall it be; for thee shall be pressed the Soma.
> Thou shalt stand as friend at my right hand;
> Then shall we slay the serried hosts of our foe."

Then a new person appears, a human singer. We know not whether a definite one among the great saints of that early time, the prophets of the later generation of singers, was thought of or not. He wished to praise Indra; but can Indra now be praised? The hostile demon is not yet conquered; doubts as to

* Rig Veda 8,100. I omit a few verses of obscure meaning, and say nothing of difficulties, for which this is not the place to give a solution.

† He is also called Vâta. This name has been identified—though the correctness of this is highly questionable—with the German name Woden.

Indra and his might come to the singer. He says to his people :

" A song of praise bring ye who long for a blessing,
If truth be truth, sing ye the praise of Indra."

" There is no Indra," then said many a one,
" Who saw him ? Who is he whom we shall praise ?"

Then Indra himself gives answer to the weak-hearted :

" Here stand I before thee, look hither, O Singer
In lofty strength I tower above all beings.
The laws of sacred order make me strong;
I, the smiter, smite the worlds."

The confidence of the pious in their God is restored, his hymn of praise is sounded. And now Indra enters the conflict. The falcon has brought him the Soma, and in the intoxication of the ambrosial drink, the victorious one hurls his thunderbolt at the demon. Like a tree smitten by lightning, falls the enemy. Now the waters may flow forth from their prisons :

" Now hasten forth ! Scatter thyself freely !
He who detained thee is no more.
Deep into the side of Vitra has been hurled
The dreaded thunderbolt of Indra.

" Swift as thought sped the Falcon along;
Pierced into the citadel, the brazen.
And up to heaven, to the thunderer,
The soaring falcon bore the Soma.

" In the sea the thunderbolt rests,
Deep engulfed in the watery billows.
The flowing and ever-constant waters
To him bring generous gifts."

I pass over the difficult conclusion of the poem—the creation of language by Indra after the battle with Vitra. One fourth of the languages that exist on earth, Indra formed into clear and intelligible speech ; these are the languages of men. The other three fourths, however, have remained indistinct and incomprehensible; these are the languages that quadrupeds and birds and all insects speak.

This is one of the early narratives of the Hindus concerning the deeds of their gods and heroes. We must not endeavor here, to restore the lost portions written in prose which served to connect the strophes. To make the modern reader clear as to the connection of the verses, another method of expression must be chosen than that peculiar to the narrators of the Vedic epoch. As it appears, they were content with recounting the necessary facts, or rather with recalling them to their hearers, in short and scanty sentences.

The verses set in the narrative are not wanting, however, in flights of poetic eloquence—as the poem of Indra's battle will have shown. Without the finer shades of human soul-life, it is true, yet in earnest simple greatness, like mountains or old gigantic trees, the heroic figures of these ancient sagas stand forth. What takes place among them is similar, nay more than similar, to that which takes place in nature. For as yet the primitive *natural* significance of those gods has hardly been veiled by the human vesture which they wear, and in the narratives of their deeds the great pictures of nature's life with its wonders and terrors are everywhere present. The duty of bringing together and interpreting such fragments of this most ancient Epic activity, Vedic investigators must reckon among their most fruitful though perhaps not their easiest tasks.

IV.

At this stage of our inquiry, the question arises, What do we know of the history of India in the age which produced the Vedas? Where does the possibility here begin of fixing events chronologically? In that part of the province of history in which this precision is lacking, can any determinate lines of another sort be drawn?

Of a history of ancient India in the sense in which we speak of the history of Rome, or in the manner in which the history of the Israelitic nation is recounted in the Old Testament, the Vedas afford us no testimony. A succession of events clearly united with one another, the presence of energetic personalities, whose aspirations and achievements we can understand, momentous struggles for the institution and security of civil government—these are things of which nothing is told to us. We may add that these are things which seem to have existed in Ancient India less than in any other civilized nation. The more we know of the history of this people the more it appears like an incoherent mass of chance occurrences. These occurrences are wanting in that firm bearing and significant sense which the power of a willing and conscious national purpose imparts to its doings. Only in the history of thought, and especially of religious thought, do we tread, in India, upon solid ground. Of a history in any other sense we can here scarcely speak. And a people who has no history, has of course no written historical works.

In those eras in which, among soundly organized nations, interest in the past and its connection with the struggles and sufferings of the present awakes, when the Herodotuses and Fabiuses, the narrators of that which has happened, are wont to arise, the literary activity of India was absorbed in theological and philosophical speculation. In all occurrences was seen but one aspect, namely, that they were transitory; and everything transitory was recognized, we may not say as a simile, yet as something absolutely worthless, an unfortunate nothing, from which the sage was bound to divert his thoughts.

We can thus easily see how fully we must renounce our hopes of an exact result, when the question is raised as to the time to which the little we know of the outer vicissitudes of the ancient Hindu tribes must be assigned, and, especially, as to the time in which the great literary remains of the Veda and the changes which it wrought in the Hindu world of thought belong. The basis that might serve toward definitely answering these questions of chronology—lists of kings with statements of the duration of each reign—is wholly wanting for the Vedic period. Of early times at least no such lists have been handed down to us; there are no traces indeed that such ever existed. The later catalogues, however, which have been fabricated in the shops of the Indian compilers, can today no more be taken into consideration as the basis of earnest research, than the statements of the Roman chroniclers as to how many years King Romulus and King Numa reigned. How unusual it was in the Vedic times for the Hindus to ask the "when" of events, is shown very clearly by the fact, that no expression was in current use by which any year but the present was distinguishable from any other year.

The result of this for us, and likewise, of course, for the science of Ancient India, is that those long centuries were and are practically synonymous with immeasurable time. The standard by which we are accustomed to compute the distance of historical antecedence in our thoughts or imaginations, fail us in this richly developed civilization as completely as in the prehistoric domains of the stone age, — in the first feeble glimmerings of human existence. In fact, as prehistoric research tries to compute the duration of the past ages which have given to the earth's surface its form, so as to determine approximately the age of the human remains embedded in the strata of the earth; so, in a similar way, the investigation of the Hindu Vedas, in its attempts to compute the age of the Veda, has sought refuge in the gradual changes that have imperceptibly taken place in the course of centuries, in that great time-measurer, the starry heavens.

There was found in a work, classed as one of the Vedas, an astronomical statement which has served as a basis for such computations. The result attained was that this particular work dated from the year 1181 B. C. (according to another reckoning 1391 B. C.). Unfortunately, the belief that in this way certain data are to be acquired had to vanish quickly enough. It was soon found out that the Vedic statement is not sufficient to afford any tenable basis for astronomical computations. Thus it remains that for the times of the Vedas there is no fixed chronological date. And to any one who knows of what things the Hindu authors were wont to speak, and of what not, it will be tolerably certain, that even the richest and most unexpected discoveries of new texts, though they may vastly extend our knowledge in other respects, will in this respect make no changes whatever.

There are two great events in the history of India with which this darkness begins to be dispelled—the one approximately, and the other accurately, referable to an ascertainable point of time. These are the advent of Buddha and the contact of the Hindus with the Greeks under Alexander the Great and his successors.

That it was the old Buddhistic communities in India that first began the work of gathering up the connected traditions within historical memory, seems certain. At least this corresponds with the apparent and accepted course of events. To Vedic and Brahmanical philosophy all earthly fortunes were absolutely worthless—a vanity of vanities; and over against them stood the significant stillness of the Eternal, undisturbed by any change. But for the followers of Buddha, there was a point at which this Eternal entered the world of temporal things, and thus there was for them a piece of history which maintained its place beside or rather directly within their religious teachings. This was the history of the advent of Buddha and the life of the communities founded by him.

There is a firm recollection of the assemblies in which the most honored and learned leaders of the communities, and great bands of monks coming together from far and wide, determined weighty points of doctrine and ritual. The kings under whom these councils were held are named, and the predecessors of these kings are mentioned even as far back as the pious King Bimbisara, the contemporary and zealous protector of Buddha. Of the series of kings which in this way have been fixed by the chronicles of the Buddhistic order, two figures are especially prominent—*Tschandragupta* (*i. e.*, the one protected by the Moon) and his grandson *Asoka* (the Painless). *Tschandragupta* is a personality well known to Greek and Roman historians. They call him *Sandrokyptos*, and relate that after the death of Alexander the Great (in the year 323 B. C.), he successfully opposed the power of the Greeks on their invasion into India, and lifted himself from a humble position to that of ruler of a wide kingdom. *Asoka*, on the other hand, is not mentioned by the Greeks; but in one of his inscriptions—by him were made the oldest inscriptions discovered in India, and these have been found on walls and pillars in the most distant parts of the peninsula—he himself speaks of Antijoka, king of the Iona (Ionians, *i. e.*, Greeks), Antikina, Alikasandara, and other Greek monarchs.*

Here at last a place is reached where the historical investigator of India reaches firm ground. Events whose years and centuries—as though they occurred on another planet—are not commensurable with those of the earth, meet at this point with spheres of events which we know and are able to measure. If we reckon back from the fixed dates of Tschandragupta and Asoka to Buddha—and we have no grounds for regarding the statements of time which we find respecting Buddhistic chronology as not at least approximately correct—we find the year of the great teacher's death to be about 480 B. C. His work therefore falls in the time at which the Greeks fought their battles for freedom from Persian rule, and the fundamental lines of a republican constitution were drawn in Rome.

Buddha's life, however, marks the extreme limit at which we may find even approximate dates. Beyond this, through the long centuries which must have

*Antijoka is Antiochas Theos; Antikina, Antigonos Gonatos; Alikasandara, of course, not Alexander the Great, but Alexander of Epirus, son of Pyrrhus, the enemy of the Romans. All these princes reigned about the middle of the third century B. C. Of Alexander the Great in India no traces have been found, with the exception of a coin which bears his picture and his name.

elapsed from the beginning of the Rig Veda epoch to that of Buddha, the question still remains: What was the succession of events—the few events of which we may speak? What the order in which the great strata of literary remains were formed? We observe the relation which one text bears to the others which appear to have previously existed; we follow the gradual changes which the language has suffered, the blotting out of old words and forms and the appearance of new ones; we count the long and short syllables of the verses so as to learn the imperceptible but strictly regular course by which their rhythms have been freed from old laws of construction and subjected to new forms; moving in a parallel direction with these linguistic and metrical changes we note the changes of religious ideas, and of the contents as well as the external forms of intellectual and spiritual life. Thus we learn in the chaos of this literature ever more surely to distinguish the old from the new, and understand the course of development which has run through both.

Many a path, it is true, in which research hoped to press forward, has been shown to be delusive and worthless; problems have had to be given up, changed, and presented in different forms. But in its last results the work has not been in vain. For, in respect to the Veda in particular, and the antiquities of India in general, we have learned to recognize the principal directions in which the tendencies of historical growth are to be traced.

From the second century of Hindu research we can scarcely expect discoveries similar to those which the first has brought: such a sudden uprising of unusual, broad, fruitful fields of historical knowledge. But we may still hope that the future of our science will bring results of another sort no less rich—the explanation of hitherto inexplicable phenomena, the transformation of that which is half known into that which is fully known.

THE RELIGION OF THE VEDA.

OUT of all the rack and ruin of Indian antiquity, the most momentous objects, which the investigator can hope to render comprehensible to the modern reader, are the great religions of ancient India. At their head stands the religion embodied in the literature of the Veda—a belief closely related to the ancient religions of the principal European peoples, but retaining in a clearer manner than they the marks of distant prehistoric stages, the traces of mighty commotions in which man's religious thought and feeling laboriously struggled forth from the crude confusion of primitive ages to nobler and more elevated forms. The religion of the Veda is in its turn replaced by the teaching of Buddha,—the one, the sternly practical religion of conquering shepherd-chieftains and their priests, the other, the world-renouncing doctrine of salvation-seeking monks. Far-reaching analogies interweave the ideals, for which the followers of the Shâkya's son forsook their homes for a life of wandering, with thoughts evolved in the Western world, especially in Greece. It seems practicable to reduce this development of the religious nature, proceeding as it did in parallel directions among peoples so widely separated, to a single general formula, that would set forth the agreement of the various powerful impulses working among them.

It will, I trust, be permitted a fellow worker in the exploration of these domains, to describe and to appraise the value of the attempts which science has made, and is yet making, to interpret these primeval monuments of human searching, longing, hoping, and to assign to them their proper place in history. But dare he make the attempt to conjure forth the figures themselves of that prehistoric world, those rare ones of silver, and with them the more numerous throng of inferior metal: can he succeed in fixing them, even though he leave the outlines somewhat doubtful and obscure?

I.

The gods and myths of earliest India became accessible to research when the latter possessed itself of the Rig-Veda, a collection of more than a thousand hymns—the great majority of them sacrificial hymns. I have described in the introductory essay of this volume, how the knowledge of the Rig-Veda was acquired, and how by hard but rapid philological work its obscurities were surely and steadily overcome. A feeling of awe was involuntarily felt on reading those poems, the antiquity of whose language loomed far beyond the old Sanskrit of even the law-book of Manu, or of the great Indian epics. A sensation, as of being led back into the deepest past of our own Teutonic ancestors, as of catching faint traces of their heart-beats in the first dawn of their antiquity, was quite generally felt, as those gods of a blood-related people arose before us; *Agni*, fire, the genial guest of human habitations; *Indra*, the thundering dragon-slayer, who uses his boundless strength to free the waters from their prison; *Varuna*, in whom it was believed the all-embracing heavens were personified, the observer and avenger of even the most hidden sins; *Ushas*, the lovely morning-blush, the dawn, who usurps the sway of her sister, the night, and, with a herd of ruddy cattle in her train traverses the firmament over, lavishing benefits and blessings.

It so happened, in the progress of science, that the first glances, which fell upon these apparitions of the gods, starting up thus suddenly from the midst of a desolated field, were the glances of comparative philologists: the same savants, who, leaping from one triumph to another, were at that very time engrossed with the work of illuminating the Greek, Latin, and Germanic inflexions with the light coming from the Sanskrit. What could be more natural than that those investigators should apply to mythology the same critical method of comparison which had borne such rich and abundant fruits in Grammar? that they should seek to establish between the divinities of the Veda and those of ancient Europe the same kinship, the same identity of origin, as existed between certain forms of Indian and Greek verbs, for example between the Indian *dadâmi* and the Greek *didômi*, both of which mean "I give"? And so, there grew up—one might say, as a branch of comparative philology—a comparative mythology, which uniformly placed the philological points of view foremost; and which placed special reliance upon the *names* of the divinities or demons, and then sought to establish their primal natures by means of an etymological treatment of these names.

In the pursuit of this course, as between the Veda and the European traditions, the leading part fell naturally enough to the former. For the Veda had the benefit of all that prestige which the Sanskrit then enjoyed in philological matters, of being the chiefest witness as to what was the first form and the first meaning of words. Why the word *daughter* should be *thygatêr* in Greek and *Tochter* in German, neither the Greek nor the German language could explain. But the Sanskrit *did* seem able to explain it. The history of the Sanskrit word for *daughter* seemed written on its very front. Since this word fell under the root *duh* (to milk), it seemed obvious that the *daughter* was originally the *milker*—a domestic idyl from remotest antiquity. And at length there was a sort of conviction, trailing at the hand of an etymology dominated by the Sanskrit, that we could, to repeat an expression of Max Müller's, reach back into regions of the past so far as to believe ourselves listening to the very voices of the earth-born sons of Manu.

It was in fact unavoidable, that this scientific art, whilst pursuing its labors with such ardor, such rich hopes, such confidence, should at the same time experience within itself the calling and the capacity, to expound, with the help of a catalogue of Sanskrit roots, the primal meaning of the hitherto mysterious divinities of Homer, of ancient Italy, and of the Edda. And it must be admitted, too, that a few of these comparisons and elaborations of the names of the old divinities really forced themselves upon the mind with overpowering conviction, and remain at this day as convincing as they were then.

But with the attempt to press on beyond this very scanty store, an approach was ever more closely made to a procedure the subjective character of which seriously endangered the security of the results already acquired. From the endless wealth of mythological names, of which the Veda is literally full, the sharp scent of the investigators hunted out and brought to light here and there a word, which, while it may have had some small resemblance to a Greek name, still occurred but rarely in the Vedic tradition. Or if there were no proper noun for the divinity to be found in the Vedic, they would fasten upon a mere adjective. Or, indeed, instead of a word actually transmitted in the Veda, they would now and then upon their own responsibility build up a Vedic word as a counterpart to the name of a Greek divinity.

Thus, in a very obscure verse of the Rig-Veda there appears a goddess, a female demon, *Saranjus*, of whose nature the Veda reveals next to nothing at all; it was thought that the primitive* form of the Greek Erinys had been found. The name Saranjus, according to its derivation from a root *sar* (to hurry), seems to mean "the hurrying one"; and the view was accordingly adopted, that she was the personification of the stormy thunder-cloud. And when the Greeks speak of Erinys as "walking in the mist," of her swinging torches in her hands, immediately plain confirmation was therein discerned for the proposition that the Erinyes, too, sprang from the conception of the thunder-cloud; their torches are the thunder-bolts which strike down the impious.

The Rig-Veda speaks of a goddess Sarama, a dog,

* Not "primitive" in the sense that the Greek goddess was derived from the Indian, but in the sense that the Indo-European prototype, common alike to the Greek and the Indian form, in all essential respects was correctly represented in the Indian form. To properly appreciate the equating of the names Saranjus and Erinys (so, too, that of Saramejas—Hermeias [Hermes]), it is to be observed that the initial *S* of Indo-European words, which was retained in Sanskrit (as also in the Latin and Teutonic), became in the Greek, when followed by a vowel, either a mere aspirate or disappeared altogether; thus our *seven* (Latin, *septem*) in Greek is written *hepta*.

who tracks the ruddy cows of the gods to their concealment when stolen; her sons, who also have canine shapes and appear to play the part of genii of sleep and death, are named after their mother Saramejas. It was thought that the Greek *Hermes* and *Hermeias* had been discovered here, the guide of souls into the realm of death, the dream-sending god of sleep. And here again the same root *sar* (to hurry) seemed to conduct the mythological interpreter into the realm of the agitated atmosphere, just as in the case of Erinys. *Sarama*, "the hurrying one," was explained as the wind; to the fleetness of the wind the dog-form of the goddess and her children seemed to correspond, in the natural symbolism of the myth.

But the wind is not the only thing in nature which moves hurriedly. And hence other interpretations were possible. *Sarama*, who recovers the treasure of ruddy cows lost in the darkness, could she not mean the morning-blush, the dawn? And does not her name appear to resemble the name of Helena? In that case, the story of the Iliad is found again in one of the standing themes of the Veda-hymns; the siege of Troy would be but a repetition of the daily siege by the martial forces of the sun, of the entrenchments of night, where the treasures of light are locked up.

Besides Helen, there appeared in the Greek a whole list of goddesses representing the Indian morning, the foremost of which was disclosed in the Vedic title of the dawn, *Ahana*. Here, it was thought, lay the germ from which the Greek Athene had sprung, the daughter of Zeus, just as in the Veda the dawn was called the daughter of Djaus, or Heaven.

In conclusion, one more of these Indo-Greek combinations may be cited: the one which of them all perhaps fared with the best luck. A part of the ancient Indian fire-drill, namely, the stick which was kept turning to ignite the wood by its friction, was called *pramantha*. Here was revealed, so it was thought, the nature of the Titan form of Prometheus. The friend of mankind—who brought to them, despite of Zeus, fire, the fountain of all art—seemed here to be announced in his original character as a divine "rubber of fire," who afterwards brings down the flame, which he has himself produced, to the earth.

It is evident that in nearly all of these combinations one characteristic regularly recurs: the origin of the divine beings, including those which appear most unequivocally to represent ethical forces or influences active in human culture, is traced back to the powers of nature. Erinys was the dark storm-cloud before she undertook the office of avenging the misdeeds of men. But in the great realm of nature there were two regions in which these interpretations of the meaning of divinities and myths lingered with particular predilection: the phenomena of storm and thunder on the one hand, and on the other the alternation of light and darkness.

At this point the leanings of investigators diverged. The question was much discussed as to which of the two classes must have produced the deepest and most lasting impressions upon the soul of youthful mankind,—those extraordinary, and, as it were, convulsive commotions which agitate the atmosphere, or the calm majesty of the divine powers of light, daily recurring with uniform grandeur.

Adalbert Kuhn was the first among those investigators who peopled the mythological landscape with storm-gods, cloud-nymphs, and demons of lightning.

He believed that the language of many myths was to be interpreted as descriptions of meteorological phenomena, the details of which—the various motions of rising, departing, scattering dark clouds, and of brighter little clouds—seemed to have been seized and expatiated upon with painful exactitude through whole lists of varying phases. According to Max Müller, on the other hand, the main theme of the Indo-Germanic myths found expression in the words *dawn* and *sun*. To his poetically attuned imagination the ancient poets and thinkers stood revealed as daily descrying in what we call sunrise the mystery of all mysteries. The dawn was to them that unknown land from whose impenetrable depths life ever newly flashes forth. The dawn opens to the sun her golden gates, and whilst her gates thus stand ajar, eyes and hearts yearn and struggle to peer beyond the limits of this finite world; the thought of the unending, the undying, the divine, awakens in the human soul. But whether storm or sunrise, all concurred in the view that in the Veda lay the guide which would conduct us to the theogony of the Indo-European peoples,—that there was here a system of religion to the last degree primal in character, clear and transparent, all the varying forms of which plainly took root in the primitive views and expressions of man upon the powers and processes of nature. As Max Müller put it, the mythological sphynx here reveals her secret; we can just barely throw a glance behind the scenes upon the forces whose play, upon Greek soil, achieved that splendid stage-effect, the majestic drama of the Olympian gods. A new direction of inquiry seemed to have opened to science, leading by undreamt-of paths to the farthest past in the life of the human soul.

Those who first broke through these paths must indeed have been possessed to an unnatural degree by indifference and suspicion, had not a kind of intoxication overwhelmed them as they confronted this plenitude of history,—if they had not experienced the hope that in the Veda they might with one bold grasp succeed in seizing the origin of myths and of very religion herself, *zu schauen alle Wirkenskraft und Samen.*

Have all these results—a lasting achievement, as it was supposed—avoided the fate of annihilation?

II.

An attack upon the teachings of comparative mythology, upon the belief in the *primitive* character of the world of Vedic gods and legends, was slowly preparing. It came, on the one hand, from the advances made in philological investigations, which stripped one supposed certainty after another of its plausible glitter. It came, on the other, from a more material opposition: the speculations, the criticisms, the discoveries, of a newly sprouting but sturdy offshoot of science, ethnology.

We shall inquire first how the art of manipulating those philological problems deepened, upon which pretty nearly everything as taught by comparative mythology depended.

In the comparison of Indian words with the Greek or Germanic a tendency arose to be severer, more suspicious, more deliberate. And with good reason. Greater circumspection was observed in applying a principle, theretofore too frequently neglected, of first subjecting the word—before undertaking to draw parallels between it and words of another tongue—to a thorough consideration within the domain of its own language, and to an examination of it in all its connexions there, throughout the whole circle of words related to it. And then, afterward, when the boundaries of the several great lingual families *were* crossed and the attempt made to bridge over the wide clefts between their respective vocabularies by means of their resemblances, it was insisted upon, with a stringency unknown to the earlier period, that a proper regard should be paid to *individual* sounds and their equivalent individual sounds in the kindred languages; correspondences which about this time began to be reduced to laws of a more and more unerring character. The mere external resemblance of words was no longer worth considering—that was something subjective and only a subjective estimate could be passed upon it. Now, the certain, unchangeable conditions were known, in obedience to which the vocal sounds of the parent Indo-European tongue have developed into the Sanskrit or the Greek or the Teutonic. Of all the comparisons made between mythological names, as alluded to, only a small minority could pass an examination so severe, but so necessary, as was now applied to them. In a word, it is flatly impossible that Prometheus should be the same word as the Indian *pramantha*; nor can Helena be the same as Sarama, for the simple reason that the Greek *n* and the Indian *m* are not equivalent.

And just as it resulted in these word-comparisons, so too the practice, once pursued with such confidence, of tracing words of different languages to roots, which were taken from the capacious granary of Sanskrit roots, proved more questionable in its character the longer it was continued. The conviction grew that instead of yielding to the dangerous temptation to read the whole origin and history of a word, or of a concept, from a few consonants, the coldest restraint ought more properly to be exercised ; and that in thousands of cases it was necessary to resignedly accept a word as a fixed quantity, as the proper name of such and such a mythological being, without endeavoring to practise that dangerous art upon it of detecting only too easily and everywhere a sunrise or a storm-cloud. In a word : it grew daily more evident that an endeavor had been made to learn too quickly, too much from *words*, and that it was high time to examine *things* instead of words, to explore with greater patience, less prejudice, the great concrete world of religious and mythological ideas, instead of guessing about them and in reliance upon doubtful etymologies imposing upon them a meaning which really and at bottom originated in the close atmosphere of the library.

But let no misunderstanding arise. It is by no means my purpose to maintain that it was not a justifiable effort on the part of investigation, to get at the common inheritance from the pre-historic Indo-European ages, by a comparison of the Indian, Greek, and German gods and legends, and thus, if possible, to enable the ideas of the respective peoples to mutually clear up and illumine both their source and their bearing. Experience alone can tell what success is to be attained in this way. But the measure of that success —though by no means wholly negative—has thus far justified but very modest expectations, if we consider such hasty results of this period as that by which *Prometheus* and *pramantha* were regarded equivalent.

In this direction, investigation achieved results almost as barren as its purely philological fruits were abundant. As to the latter, it has in the main restored the paradigms of the Indo-Germanic language by the comparison of Indian, Greek, Latin, Germanic, and Slavic declensions and conjugations, and in the same way gotten at the processes by which the parent paradigms became transmuted into the paradigms of the filial tongues; and it has accomplished this with evidences of growing confidence, since its successes all the while steadily augmented in volume—and this is the surest proof that the course pursued has been the correct one.

The reason is manifest. The variations in forms, of *grammatical* systems, are the product of factors relatively simple, which, for the most part, can be expressed in formulæ of almost mathematical certainty. In mythological history, on the contrary, a throng of varying influences are all at once in play, so complex and so involved that the glance in vain may seek to comprehend them all at once. A certain group of ideas at one time fades away and disappears, anon they collect again, gather closely, and again assume a definite concrete form. Elements, once widely separated, later on meet and form new combinations, which, in their turn, in the endeavor to assume a finished form, or to maintain themselves at all, are compelled to give forth new ideas, offshoots of themselves. Mental processes, which are unconsciously conducted, intersect with conscious cerebrations of primitive poesy and speculation, the motives of which frequently are far removed and accessible only with great difficulty to modern habits of thought. And finally external interests, too, play their part: emulations of every kind, the struggle for property or position, vanity, and no end of other impulses of a similar character. And this chaotic confusion is lit up but sparsely, in spots, by the murky light of tradition, and with this light, only, science has to work. Between these dimly lighted spots are boundless expanses lying in deepest gloom; so that when the thread once slips from the hand of the investigator, he is greatly in danger of losing himself altogether.

It is therefore easy to comprehend that the attempt to bridge over the vast distance between India on the one hand, and Greece or the Teutonic world on the other, has infinitely poorer chances of success in things pertaining to religions and legend than in the case of mere inflexions. Still, when all is said, there is no lack of specific instances where this comparison of Indian and European divinities has succeeded in spite of the difficulties presented. The twins *Asvin*, literally "the horsemen," those radiant young divinities, who speed across the vault of heaven at early morn with their fleet chariot and to the oppressed appear as deliverers from every kind of suffering, certainly correspond—of this I am firmly convinced—to the Greek *Dioskuroi*, as well as afford assistance in getting at the nature of the *Dioskuroi*. *Indra*, the strongest of the Vedic divinities, who, hurling his weapon, slays the dragon and liberates the imprisoned waters, is truly the same god as Thor in the Edda, the dragon-fighter, the hammer-hurler.[1] Both in India and in the Teutonic

[1] Note that both in the comparison Indra=Thor, as well as in that of Asvin=Dioskuroi, the names fail philologically to agree. As remarked before, the attempt has been made to draw a parallel between the Greek Hermes and the Indian dog-divinity Sarameyas. Hermes really belongs, with greater show of reason, to a classification with the Vedic god Pushan, who, like Hermes, rules as protector over roads and travellers, like him is the messenger of the gods, and acts as escort of souls into the future life, and like Hermes protects herds and reveals lucky treasures. The juxtaposition of the material qualities of ideas thus leads to results absolutely independent of any assistance to be gotten from the etymological comparison of names.

north the storm-god of the Indo-Europeans has preserved a uniformity of nature which is at once recognisable. But, to repeat, the stock of such comparisons which can safely be maintained, is a very modest one, and we hardly have reason to form hopes of obtaining greater successes of this sort in the future than we have obtained in the past.

III.

More decisive than the reformation accomplished within philology itself, the course of which we traced in the last section, was the influence on Vedic research of a new class of inquiries, which were far removed from the domain of comparative philology and of Sanskrit, and which tended to overthrow altogether the belief that the Veda was the representative type of every primitive religion and mythology. We refer to the researches of the comparative ethnologists who were now making a highly comprehensive and systematic study of the elusive forms which the religious sentiment, the cult, the myth-creating phantasy of modern peoples assumed in the lower and the lowest stages of civilisation.

And here a discovery of the utmost import was made, the honors of which belong first of all to English investigators such as Tylor and Lang, and along with them to an excellent German scholar, Wilhelm Mannhardt. It was found that, very much like their weapons and utensils, so too the religion of the lowest orders of man, the whole world over, was everywhere one and the same in its essential elements. By some intrinsic necessity, there is always imposed upon this low state of evolution just this particular type of ideas and customs, which is the normal one, and as such may be looked for with absolute certainty.

This type of belief and cult, which is only faintly idealistic, and is dominated by thoroughly harsh and practical views, we shall describe at some length farther on. At this point we have simply to remark upon the evident conclusion to be drawn from these observations, that the ancestors, also of those peoples, which we meet with in historic times as the possessors of most opulent civilisations, must, in some prehistoric age, however remote, have gone through just such a savage period of religious and ritualistic development.

This fact established, there was at once opened to scholars who did not deem it beneath them to learn something from American Indians, negroes, and Australians, a source of highly important data drawn directly from the mouths of living witnesses, by which it was possible to reveal prehistoric epochs antedating even the Homeric or Vedic religions, and preparatory to them. Reasoning from the ideas of modern savages, to the ideas obtaining in the prehistoric savage state of subsequently civilised peoples, may have seemed a hazardous undertaking; but there was a sure corrective for the procedure. It is well-known that in all transitions of lower civilisations to higher, many elements of the old condition persist and hold over in the new, and that the spirit of the new can neither destroy nor assimilate them. They persist as *survivals* of the past in the midst of altered surroundings, and are absolutely unintelligible to people who know only the tendency and ways of the new period; they can be explained only from the point of view of the time in which they originated—a time when they were active principles,—a time, the tracks of which they preserve, as it were, in a fossil condition.

Now if our view is correct, such survivals must be found at every step in a mythology and a cult like the Veda—and, we might likewise say, in the mythology and cult of Homer; they must be the special lurking-places of whatever appears to be irrational, odd, self-contradictory, and difficult of exposition. But, on the other hand, whatever in those poems seems incomprehensible to the man of to-day must become intelligible as soon as the art is acquired of looking at it from the standpoint of the modern savage and with the help of his peculiar logic, both of which are often totally distinct from ours.

As a matter of fact, the moment a search was made through the ancient Indian and the related European civilisations for such remains of prehistoric and anticipatory culture, the conviction forced itself irresistibly on scholars that the correct method had at last been discovered. Problems quickly resolved themselves, which theretofore dared scarcely be approached. The most striking agreements were disclosed between the various types of myth and cult scattered at this very day over the earth among our savages and barbarians, and the type of myth and cult which had lain imbedded in the Veda as a mass of unintelligible facts, wholly irreconcilable with any interpretation derived from the known intellectual character of the Vedic world.

The chain of proof was thus rendered continuous and conclusive. Science had succeeded (or at least was steadily advancing toward success)—not by means of bare grammatical speculations or the study of Sanskrit roots, but by inquiries which rested at every point upon a basis of living fact—in showing that there was a certain elementary state at the beginning of all civilisations and in disclosing the gray, early dawn anticipatory of the broad daylight of their history. This was a revelation, which—however gradually and modestly it asserted itself—is perhaps of even farther-reaching importance in the exploration of antiquity than those brilliant exploits of the philologist's finished art which has opened the way to the remote recesses of Egyptian and Babylonian civilisation.

As a result of this discovery, a place was given to the religion and mythology of the Veda widely different from that which the enthusiasm of its earlier students had sought to assign to them. The assumption that the Veda revealed the secret of the elementary formative processes of creed and cult, was thus shown to be as far wide of the mark, as it would have been to have considered the grammar of the Sanskrit, the complexity of which points to an infinitely long preparatory history, as the elemental grammar of human speech. The fact is, it is not true, as the supposition had been up to that time, that the myth-building phantasy of man is revealed in its natural processes in the Veda, as plainly as a clock housed in glass reveals all its wheels and works. The Vedic divinities, the Vedic sacrifices, are not primitive and transparent products of the original creative force of religion, but for the most part turn out, on close scrutinisation, to be ancient, obscure, and complex creations.

We shall next attempt a description of the age preceding the Vedic religion, and also of that religion itself, as both appear from the point of view here sketched.*

* I have given this subject a more detailed treatment in my book *The Religion of the Veda.* (1894.)

IV.

THE fundamental nature of the primary Indian religion, surviving from the very remotest antiquity and rising to the surface of the Vedic times as a more or less ruinous wreckage, is, as we have seen, essentially that of the savage's religion. According to this, all existence appears animated with spirits, whose confused masses crowd upon each other, buzzing, flocking, swarming along with the phantom souls of the dead, and act, each according to its nature, in every occurrence. If a human being fall ill, it is a spirit that has taken possession of him and imposes upon him his ills. The patient is cured by enticing the spirit from him with magic. A spirit dwells in the flying arrow. He who shoots off an arrow performs a bit of magic which puts this spirit into action. The spirits have sometimes human, sometimes animal form. Neither form is nobler or lower than the other, for as yet no distinction between the human and bestial nature has been made. In fact, man is usually looked upon as descended from the animal; the tribes of men are called bears, wolves, snakes, and the individuals of the animal genus after which they are thus called are treated by the tribes as their blood-relations.

As they move hither and thither, the spirits may select a domicile, abiding or temporary, in some visible object. A feather, or a bone, or a stone at different times holds the spirit; and anon the spirit steals into a human being whom it makes ill, or throws into convulsions in which supernatural visions come to him and in which the spirit talks through him in confused phrases.

And just as man at this stage of development lives only for the moment, thrown unresistingly to and fro by all sorts of vacillatory influences, such naturally is the way of the spirits. The spirits of savages are themselves savages, greedy, superstitious, easily excitable. The man of skill, the magician, who as yet occupies the place filled at a later period by the priest, knows the art—first anticipatory hints of a cult—of flattering the spirits; he understands how to bar their passage, to terrify them, to deceive them, to compel them, to provoke them against his enemy. They are washed away with water; they are consumed by fire; even the friendly spirits, whenever they prove themselves intractable, are subjected to the same sort of irreverent treatment. It is apparent that this religion knows of nothing possessing a majesty which at all rises above the level of human life. An appreciation, an estimate of differences of magnitude and of degree have not as yet been formed. Animal, man, spirit, are mixed up together, all more or less equal in their power and in their rights.

But gradually the chaos of these ideas clarifies. The great begins to separate itself from the little, the noble from the base. A calmer survey of the world obtains.

And so, out of all the confusion of forces working in the shape of spirits, the great powers of nature more and more emerge and assume the first position. Their action, reaching far beyond human control into the farthest regions of space, the same to-day as yesterday and to-morrow as to-day, invincible to all human opposition, is ever more felt to be decisive of destinies; —the more so, as the various branches of human industry (cattle breeding and agriculture) make improvement and hence intensify man's sensitiveness to the favorable and unfavorable phenomena of nature. It is, therefore, the normal characteristic of vast stretches of historical development that the great powers of nature, such as the heavens, sun, moon, storm, thunder, and with these the terrestrial element of fire and the earth itself (usually first in importance in this class), appear as the highest givers of blessings and rulers of all that happens. They are superior to man and are at a distance from him, as befits divinity. For the embodiment of them into a living personification, the more perfect form of man steadily secures the preference over that of the brute. It was only possible to deify the torpid brute so long as man failed to feel himself as something better than the brute.

Of course the animal figure does not disappear absolutely and at a single blow from the midst of the divinities. Subordinate divinities, standing in the background and thus remaining untouched by the ennobling tendencies, were allowed to retain their old animal form. Or, an animal, which was once itself a god, might, after the god had been exalted to the dignity of human form, remain to the latter as a special attribute, as a sort of celestial domestic animal,—as, for illustration, demons which were once of the shape of horses, being raised to gods with the shape of man, would thereafter appear as riding upon celestial horses. Or, some *part* of the body of the original animal form might be retained as a part of the newer human form of the god; or something emblematic of the animal be affixed externally in some way, and thus retain a trace of the old conception which had been overthrown. And wherever a plastic art has developed established forms, as in Egypt or in Mexico, and is consequently strongly conservative in retaining venerable traditions, the animal-gods, cut in stone, may expect to maintain themselves for a longer time than they could wherever, as was the case in India in the time of the Veda, they lived in the airy realm of the imagination.

In the same manner, the practice of considering stone and wood as fetishes embodying the spirits, while not disappearing suddenly and wholly, yet unavoidably withdraws from the foreground. The spookish, magical conception of spirits slipping stealthily from one home to another in matter of every shape and kind loses ground. The figures of the divinities obtain surer forms, each with peculiar outlines of its own, and their dignity, at once human and supernatural, is firmly established. Though far from approaching to that ideal of sanctity to which a later age will attain; though they are still animated by egotism, passions, caprices of every sort,—yet, accompanying it all, a certain amount of constancy becomes manifest in them, and in all their doings there is evident the steady growth of connected deliberation and plan. Very often the tendency develops of transfering to these divinities the rôle of kindly dispensers of bounties, while, on the other hand, the occupation of doing injury, of causing illness and harm of every sort, is still allotted to inferior demons, gnomes, goblin spirits, which in their essentials keep on a level with sorcery of the earlier religion and against which the old arts of spell and exorcism are effective,—arts, which, be it observed, are of no avail against the higher power of the new great divinities.

The intercourse of man with these new gods attunes itself to another key. He is studious to gratify the immortals, powerful beings, willingly inclining themselves to favor, when approached with gifts. He invites them to food and drink and they yield to his solicitation; not, however, with the bluster and din of the spirits exorcised by the old sorcerers, but in calm grandeur the invisible gods approach their adorers. The distinctive seal, now stamped upon cult, is henceforth, and for long periods of time, sacrifice and prayer.

It is at this point that it becomes clear what the proper position of the Vedic religious belief is. Not all perhaps, but yet all the chief and dominant of the Vedic divinities are based upon a personification of natural forces, in forms of superhuman magnitude. The dwelling-place of the most of them is the atmosphere or the heavens. The word *devas* (the god), which the Indians had received from the Indo-Germanic past and which is to be found among many of the related branches of the family,* meant originally "the heavenly one." And thus the belief, which elevates the divinities above human kind to a heavenly height, was firmly fixed and long antedates the times of the Veda.

From it all, we see at the first glance that with the Veda we are dealing with a stage of development which must have been preceded by a long prior history. And we find a confirmation for such a view, which, as was explained above, might be expected in a case of this kind: the types of divinities, or rather of spirits, characteristic of more primitive stages of development, are profusely apparent throughout the world of Vedic divinities. The divinities themselves—heavenly human

*Thus, Latin: *divus*, *deus*. Ancient Gallic: *devo-*, *divo-*. Lithuanian: *dëvas*. Old Prussian: *deiwas*. Ancient Norse (in which, according to rules of consonantalchange, *t* instead of *d* appears): *tivar*, the gods

beings, exalted to a colossal magnitude, in agreement with the general religious thought of the Vedic age—retain numerous, not wholly obliterated, marks of their ancient animal form. Demons of animal shape, like "the serpent from the earth," "the one-footed goat," surround the world of man-resembling divinities, and form a back-ground for them. And the gods themselves are, in certain rites,—although exceptionally, as may be imagined,—represented fetish-like as embodied in animals, sometimes too in inanimate objects. A steed represents Agni, the fleet god of fire; an ox, Indra, who is strong as one.

Further, there are plain relics visible in the Veda of the belief so characteristic of the savage races: the belief in the blood-relationship between certain human families and certain animal species.

Again, in India as elsewhere, there appear along with the grand divinities, which are mainly beneficent and are raised by the advance of thought to purer forms, those spirits by which the savage imagines he is encircled. They are those cobolds, malicious sprites, spirits of illness, which we may say belong to the Stone Age of religion, which are obdurate to any historical growth, and yet are found with the same characteristics among all peoples; gliding about in human and animal forms and misshapes—by day and by night, but especially night—everywhere, but with a marked partiality for cross-roads, grave-yards, and other such dismal places; stealing into man, cheating him, confusing his mind, gnawing at his flesh, sucking up his blood, waylaying his women, drinking up the milk of his cows. And finally, along with these spirits, and characteristic of the same primitive notions, there appear, in the belief of the Veda, the souls of the dead,—those of ancestors kindly watching over the destinies of their children,—and treacherous, inimical souls: a domain in which the Veda has retained in especial abundance, and scarcely concealed beneath the veil spread over them by its advanced ideas, the remains of a savage and most crude religious life.

If we turn, now, from these survivals of a distant past, to the great divinities, which are characteristically the figure-heads of the religion of the Veda, we shall find that the stage at which the work of deifying the powers of the air and of the heavens is usually accomplished, has been quite appreciably passed. While these divinities, too, have sprung from early ideas of nature, the roots which they there struck have withered or are at least touched with incipient decay; the original meaning taken from nature is either forgotten or misunderstood. The mightiest of the Vedic gods, Indra, was once the thunderer, who batters open the cloud-cliffs with his weapon of lightning and frees the torrents of rain;—in the hymns of the Veda he has faded into the very different figure of the divine *hero*, physically strongest of the gods, the conferrer of victories, he who performs all the most powerful feats and lavishes inexhaustible treasures. The Vedic poets do, indeed, tell that legend of Indra, which was once the legend of the thunder, of the slaying of the serpent and the opening of the cliff; but in their recital it is all distorted. The cliff, which Indra's weapon splits, is no longer the cloud, but a literal terrestrial cliff; and the rivers which he releases are actual terrestrial rivers. The conception of thunder has thus wholly disappeared from the myth of Indra and there has only remained the story that the strongest of the gods had split a wall of rock with his marvellous weapon and that the streams had poured forth from it.

The same process of fading out has befallen a number of other of these great natural divinities. The two *Asvin*, the *Dioskuroi* of the Greeks, have lost their meaning of morning and evening star. In the Vedic creed their essential characteristic is that they are the deliverers of the oppressed from all kinds of suffering. Varuna, in his original character a lunar divinity, was transformed into that of a heavenly king, the observer and punisher of all sins; and the single characteristic, that he is the divine ruler of the night, alone shows an obscure mark of his long-forgotten real nature.

In this way the deified forces of nature were transmuted into immortal masters, and protectors of the different conditions and interests of human life. The process is readily comprehended. The lively feeling of owing everything good to the powers of nature, in itself no mean advance upon the earlier crude conceptions, unavoidably dulls with time. The growing cohesion and order of society, the more extensive character of all the enterprises of peace and war at this stage, allows new trains of ideas to press to the front. The power of the king and war-hero now forces itself upon the attention as decisive of destiny; and accordingly in those divinities who personified nature in the forms of preternatural men, the element of nature recedes more and more before the element derived from man. The suggestion of the morning star, or of the moon, pales before the stronger consciousness of being under the merciful protection or the corrective power of heroic and royal divine masters.

These divine lords, as they are pictured in the Veda, all possess strong family resemblances. They are all very powerful, very glorious, very wise, very ready in aid. They all stand out in uniformly Titanic stature, each one like his fellows, but poor in the possession of that matchless beauty in which the Greek saw his gods standing glorious before him. Zeus knits his dark brows, his ambrosial locks tumble forwards, and the Olympic heights tremble; the barbaric god of the Veda "whets his horns and shakes them powerfully like a bull," the same sort of expression as that with which an early Chaldaic hymn, standing at about the same point of evolution, says of its god, "that he lifts his horns like a wild bull." As yet, religious thought and feeling have not advanced the idea of divinity from the point of grandeur to that of infinity, from power to omnipotency, and have not in particular taken the step from multiplicity to unity.

A *single* God is created by a history like that of the Old Testament, which, in the stress of great national experiences, in triumph and in defeat, so intimately binds a people with the divinity that controls its destiny, that beside it all other gods disappear. Or, a *single* God may be created by reflexion seeking over and beyond the heights and depths of existence the one loftiest height or the one inmost germ of all things. The former is the god of heroes and patriots; the latter the still, calm divinity of the solitary speculator. But the bards of the Veda were neither patriots nor philosophers. The peace and comfortable existence of ancient India, the dispassionate character of the popular soul, to which a deep and intense attachment to its own national existence remained unknown, were but rarely disturbed by national misfortunes or passions such as those with which the history of Israel is filled.* And that impulse of philosophical reflexion toward unity in the confusion of phenomena is as yet foreign to the age whose religious beliefs we are here describing. Such an impulse does not begin to show itself until the time of some of the latest poems of the Rig-veda, then, however, growing in the succeeding era to irresistible strength.

The same multiplicity of gods, therefore, prevails in the Veda as of old—not the clean-cut result of a methodical partition, so to speak, of the administrative offices of the world's affairs among divine officials, but the complex product of manifold historical pro-

*To appreciate thoroughly the difference in the whole tone of historical and religious sentiment in the Veda and in the Old Testament, compare two songs which in a measure occupy corresponding positions in the two literatures—the Song of the Victory of King Suda (Rig-veda, 7, 18) and the Triumphal Song of Deborah (Judges, v). Both belong to the earliest poetical monuments—are possibly the oldest—of the nation from which they emanate. Both glorify hardly-won victories; the details of the two battles bear great resemblance to each other, so far as may be judged from the vacillating floods of the two hymns of victory. In each a swollen stream brought destruction to the foe.

But how differently does the song of the heroic-souled Jewish patriotess resound from that of the Brahmanic court-priest and poet. In the former, every word glows with passion, with a drunken joy of victory. Every whit of its energy is strained for the fight, the people staked its very soul upon the issue. Jehovah marched forth and all nature joined in the combat; the clouds deluged the earth with waters; the stars in their courses contended against Sisera. We see the hostile leader collapse before the shepherd woman, who gave him milk when he asked for water, and struck him down with her hammer. We see his mother gazing after him and moaning at the window lattice, "Why tarry the wheels of his chariots?"

How different is the atmosphere of the Indian poem! In the foreground stands the priest, busily and successfully performing his office,

> "As in pasture rich and fat the cow
> Drips milk, so Vashtha's song dripped over thee,
> O Indra! Master of the herds art thou,
> All say. Incline, accept our noblest offering."

The foe fled like cattle from the pasture when they have lost their herder. Indra struck them down the moment the votive offering was cast upon his altar; all the offered sweets he gave to Sudas to enjoy. What glimpse do we catch here of anxiety and of the outburst of prodigious passion on the part of a people battling for its existence!

cesses, of a kind of "struggle for existence" between ideas, on the one hand, whose value for the religious consciousness has dwindled away but which often maintain themselves more or less by a sheer faculty of pertinacity and those ideas which press into prominence through being favored by the advance of intellectual and material life.

A final very marked characteristic of these divinities is that the phantasy of their adorers by no means raised them to the highest level of moral majesty, as they did to positions of the greatest power and highest glory. This step of incomparable importance in the evolution of religion—the association of the ideas of God and good—as yet can be descried in but a few faint signs, and this state most surely marks the religion as still a barbaric one. At this stage, the thing most essential to the needs of the devout is that the God be a strong and kindly ruler, and of an easily influenced disposition. But how was it possible that the mighty thunderer of pre-Vedic times, or the mighty warrior and bestower of blessings of the Vedic religion, Indra, should be formed of other ethical stuff than they, whose image he was, the terrestrial *grands seigneurs*? The savage battles which fill his existence alternate with savage adventures of love and drink. Very little does he inquire into the sinfulness or rectitude of mankind; but all the more is he desirous of knowing who has slaughtered oxen on his altar and brought as an offering his favorite drink, the intoxicating soma, whose streams "pour into him as rivers into the ocean," and "fill his belly, head, and arms." And it occasionally happens that he is not over particular about remembering the wishes which his worshippers have preferred in their prayers, as when returning in the best of humor to his dwelling from a sacrifice in his honor, he says: "This is what I will do,—no, that: I'll give him a cow!—or shall it be a horse? I wonder if I have really had soma from him to drink?"

Still, if one were to contemplate the picture of the Vedic divinities from this position only, he would be apt to falsely appreciate the manifold complexity of the intermingling currents. Distinct, it may be they were, originally, from the conceptions formed of the gods, yet the ideas of right and wrong, the sympathy naturally felt with the candid and fair man, the repudiation of tortuous treachery, dread of the chains imposed by guilt whether deliberate or unintentional, all this, of course, is well known to the Vedic world, and is expressed with sufficient vivacity in the Vedic poetry. And why, indeed, should not this domain of human interests and laws also find its rulers and representatives among the heavenly beings as well as war, or man's daily occupation, or his domestic life?

Although, therefore, the Vedic divinities as such and taken as a whole manifest no special character of holiness or rectitude, properly speaking, there is among them one particular divinity, Varuna,—originally a lunar divinity, as already said,—who assumes, as peculiarly his own, the office of caring for the mundane moral order—assisted by a circle of less prominent companions, who were originally, it is possible, the sun and the planets. This moral order is looked upon as having been originally established by Varuna, and by Varuna's strong arm and sorcery it is preserved. Varuna detects even the most secret transgression; his snares are set for the treacherous; he sends forth his avenging spirits; he threatens the guilty with misfortune, illness, death. He suffers his forgiveness and pardon to shield the penitent, who make effort to appease him.

In a song of the Rig-veda, a guilt-laden one, pursued by disaster, cries: "I commune thus with myself: When may I again approach Varuna? What offering will he deign to accept, without showing anger? When shall I, my soul reviving, behold again his favor? Humbly, as a servant, will I make reparation to him, merciful that he is, that I may be once more blameless. To them that are thoughtless, the god of the Aryans has given prudence; wiser than the knowing man, he advances them to riches."

Varuna is here called the Aryan god. The historian, however, can hardly approve the bard's claim, for I believe we can discover in the apparently Aryan form of this god the signs of an un-Aryan derivation. This much at all events is certain: that faith in their chief protector of the right extends backward into the epoch when the ancestors of the Indians still formed one people with the ancestors of the Iranians, as they hesitated on the threshold of the Indian peninsula. This god appears among the Indo-Iranians as Varuna, among the Iranians (in the religion of Zoroaster) as the chief ruler of all that is good, Ahura Mazda, or Ormuzd. We cannot trace Varuna beyond the age of the Indo-Iranians into the prior time of the Indo-Europeans. Among the related peoples, like the Greeks or Teutons, we find no signs of him. Much, on the contrary, seems to me to agree in favor of the view that the Indo-Iranians had received this god from without, from the regions subject to Babylonian civilisation. If I am right in this conjecture, is it to be looked upon as merely fortuitous that right at the time when the remotest Semitic and pre-Semitic civilisation had fructified the religion of the Aryans, the point lies where the figure of the sin-avenging and sin-forgiving Varuna begins to separate from the primeval coarseness of such bruiser and tippler divinities as Indra, and to be distinguished by the sublime traits of sanctity and divine mercy?

It has been remarked that the cult devoted to divinities, at the point of the evolution of the Veda, chiefly assumes the form of the sacrifice. The gods have so far grown beyond human dimensions that the magic spells which could compel them at the will of man, no longer appear as the proper agency with which to influence them. And on the other hand, they are as yet too far removed from pure spirituality for a purely spiritual form of adoration. The worshipper may and must make himself acceptable to them by the simplest measures, industriously, loudly, even obtrusively. Resembling man as they do, they eat and drink like men. Accordingly offerings of food and intoxicating drink were needful, in order to fortify them and to stir them to mighty actions. They had to be flattered; they were to be addressed in the most artfully agreeable style, and in the most superlative expressions possible as to their grandeur and their splendor. Thereupon is the proper moment for the worshippers, who sit around the sacrificial ceremony "like flies about honey," to lay their desires before the gods: desires which—corresponding to the spirit of the age—are ever directed to the palpable goods of earthly existence,—a long life, posterity, the acquisition of property in horses and cattle, favorable weather, triumph over all enemies. The art of properly performing these sacrifices and prayers is the main theme about which the whole spiritual life of the poets of the Rig-veda revolves. To them the sacrifice is the embodiment of all mysteries, the symbol of all the most important and profound of the phenomena of life. "By means of sacrifices, the gods offered sacrifices,—those were the first of all laws," says the Rig-Veda.

The external marks of the Vedic sacrifice are so far simple, that as yet all the elements are wanting to it, which follow in the train of urban life and especially of the development of the fine arts. There are no temples, no images of the divinities. The cult of shepherd tribes, whose migratory manner of life has not yet entirely become a fixed one, is as yet satisfied with a very simple altar,—established with the same facility everywhere,—the level, cleared greensward, over which soft grass is strewn, about the holy fires, as a resting-place for the invisible gods, who quickly collect from the atmospheric regions around.

But there is no lack of artful embellishment of another kind in the Vedic sacrifice,—or even of an over-embellishment, according to Oriental custom. The song of praise and prayer, delivered at the sacrifice, is fashioned after the rules of an elaborate art, growing ever more intricate. It is overladen with obscure allusions, in which theological mysticism parades its acquaintance with the hidden depths and crannies of things divine. To utter such a prayer and to offer up such a sacrifice not every one is called or fitted whom the inner impulse moves, but only the trained priest, one belonging to certain families who have formed an exclusive spiritual caste from time immemorial,—the priest who alone is accounted equal to the perilous, sacred duty of eating of the sacrificial feast, and to drink of the soma, the intoxicating drink of the gods. At sacrificial ceremonies of greater importance priests of this kind appear in throngs, singing, reciting, and performing the immense number of prescribed acts with that painful, purely external nicety which is peculiar to every cult standing at this point of historical development, and the displacement of which by the inner soul-life is everywhere the product of protracted later evolution.

Religious ceremony of this sort is, indeed, far from having attained to the "affair of *conscience*" of the devout believer—to the elevation of a force which exalts and clarifies his inner life. It is—conducted on a large scale and with reference to human interests as a whole—simply what the cult of sorcery of an earlier age had been in a small way and with reference to some particular human want: a practice which any one, who could bear the expense, might have put into motion for himself by the skilled practitioner, to enrich one's self, to prolong life, to avert sickness and all harm.

But here there is repeated, in matters purely of cult, the same characteristic which confronted us in another connexion. Alongside of and interwoven with the formations which carry the special imprint of Vedic culture, everywhere and often in compact masses, there are the remains of hoary constructions, traceable to remoter and even to remotest times. As just remarked, it is a peculiarity of the Vedic cult of the sacrifice, that it concerns itself chiefly with human interests viewed as a whole; but still it was an unavoidable retention, that the supernatural forces should be put into action, upon occasion, for individual and particular situations, in behalf of want or suffering at some particular moment. It is here that the old witchcraft especially retained whatever was left to it of its former importance, in the Vedic age. He who wished to drive away evil spirits, or the substance supposed to have brought an illness, or, similarly, some guilt, had recourse still, as in former ages, to fire, which consumes the hostile thing, or to water which washes it away, or he chased the spirits away with din and alarms, blows and bow-shot. He who wished to produce rain, proceeded much like the rain-conjurer among the savages of our day. He put on black robes, and slew in sacrifice some black-colored beast, in order to attract the black clouds with which it was designed to cover the sky; or, he threw herbs into the water that the grass of his pastures might be splattered by the divine waters. He who wished to prepare himself for particularly holy rites, acted just as the modern savage does, when he strives to transport himself into the exalted state in which man may enjoy communion with the gods. One about to perform the sacrifice of the soma, prepared himself for his holy labor, clad in dark-colored skins, muttering in stuttering speech, fasting until "there is nothing left in him, nothing but skin and bones, till the black pupil disappears from his eye," maintaining his position beside the magic fire which frightened away the evil demons, thus producing within him the necessary condition of inner fever (*tapas*); a practice, which lies in the midst of the Vedic ritual as an unintelligible relic of by-gone ages, but which a modern American Indian or a Zulu would comprehend at once, since very similar customs are familiar to him.

Thus, the religion and the cult of the Veda point on the one hand to the past of the savage religion; on the other hand, they point forward. We have seen that the majority of the Vedic divinities had long since lost their original meaning. Indra is no more the thunderer; nor Varuna the night-illuminating planet. For a time the faded images of the powers, which were once effective in their influence upon human faith, maintain their entity by the sheer force of pertinacity —similar to a movement, which, receiving no fresh impulse, gradually dies away. The point will come at which the motion will cease. The intellect, pressing onward, recognises other forces as the effective. New exigencies of the soul require to be satisfied by other means than those proffered by the benevolence of Indra or Agni.

BUDDHISM.

HAVING in the preceding essay sought to establish the position which the earliest form of the Indian religion properly occupies in the great process of the evolution of religion, the task presents itself of attempting to fix a similar historical position for a later stage of the same growth, namely for ancient Buddhism,—one of those structures in the history of religion, which, as a complete expression of deepest content, may well be classified with the classic types of human religion and human pursuit of salvation.

I.

The prevailing mood and, even more yet, the forms of mental expression in which the thought and life of the mendicant Buddhist monks revolved possess an almost contemporary double upon Greek soil: the creations of the West and the East corresponding closely to each other to an astonishing degree, in matters the most essential as well as in the most subordinate, even to the coining of rally-words about which the religious consciousness loves to concentrate, or to the drawing of similes which aim to make the grand direction of events in some sort palpable to the imagination, and which, while apparently of inferior import, often really belong to the most powerful factors of religion.

It is plainly no mere accident that a harmony between the ideas of two people, so widely separated both in space and national characteristics, should be so much more strongly and variously accentuated, just at the period of evolution of which we are here speaking, than it was before that time. The myth-building imagination which holds sway during the earlier periods, proceeds without aim or method upon its course. It receives its impulse from chance; accident combines in it capriciously materials widely divergent in character; as if at play, accident pours into its lap, out of a copious horn, forms which are sometimes of noteworthy depth and meaning, sometimes absurd, but which are ever changing and displacing each other. But when reflexion, presently developing into sustained and systematic investigation, takes a grasp of some firmness and certainty on the problems of the cosmos and human existence, the scope of possibilities contracts. However untrained the mind may be in this age, yet the things that appear to it perforce as realities, go far to compel human ideas into a fixed and constrained course, like a stream into its bed; and thus the most manifold lineaments, showing remarkable resemblances to each other, are similarly impressed upon analogous courses of thought in widely different parts of the world, as was the case with those which preoccupied the Greek and Indian minds.

Being wholly without any knowledge as to the time-limitations of Vedic antiquity, we can hardly attempt to estimate the number of centuries lying between the origin of the Rig-Veda hymns and the rise of Buddha, the founder of the Buddhistic monastic order. But we have sufficient reason to fix the latter event as having taken place in the latter half of the sixth century before Christ. The religious movements which prepared the way for it and created a sort of Buddhistic atmosphere before the appearance of Buddha, must certainly have occupied a length of time which is to be measured by centuries. So much is certain that great historical changes occurred in India between the age of the bards who sang at the Vedic altars, and that of the Buddhistic monastic thinkers. The tribes who had originally settled as shepherds in the northwest corner of the peninsula, and who were still close to the gates by which they had shortly before entered India, had in the meantime penetrated still farther. Having taken possession of a broad domain stretching down the Ganges, the period of migration and of conquest over the obscure aborigines is over. Cities have long since risen in the midst of the villages in which had lived the herd owners of the older time,—some of them were great municipalities, seats of all the commotion and activity of splendid despotic Oriental courts, where commerce and manufactures are highly developed, where life receives zest from a voluptuously refined luxury, and where have become established sharp social differentiations of rich and poor, master and slave. The conditions have thus been prepared, where, abandoning gradually the careless and aimless existence, for the day as it were, of the earlier period, the human mind of the new period now becomes maturer and more thoughtful, may begin to weave a connected fabric of reflexions upon the import, the end, and the value of human existence.

Accordingly, in India, very similarly and at almost the same time as in Greece, edifices of spiritual thought and doctrine arise which soar to a height far above the ancient structures. And they can, indeed, be described, almost with completeness and in detail, without feeling the necessity of intermingling any distinctively Indian or Greek characteristics in the description; so much is the type developed by the one people like that developed by the other.

To the devout worshipper of the former age, communing with his god by means of sacrifice and prayer, the knowledge of his god and of the art by which the god's favor may be secured, does not appear as something self-achieved or self-created, or indeed created by any person. Rather, it is an intuition, the presence of which is a simple fact, and the possession of which by one's self as well as by every other rational being is a matter of course. But a change takes place. The intellect, as it proceeds in its experience of the toil and the pleasure of personal search, learns to know the elation of finding, the pride felt in knowledge which has been personally achieved and wrested from reality after many long and painful struggles. A man enjoys the final triumph of his vision, the keenness of which he has himself trained, and which is able to penetrate to the centre of things, differently from the masses, common-place beings, who stop at the surface of things. Among them he feels himself like one who can see among the blind.

Evidently enough, those possessed of such a vision are not sufficiently numerous to compose more than small knots of thinkers made up of the serious kind, of those whose sentiments are of the more delicate or refined sort, of those who cultivate their inner life with more than ordinary zeal. In the bosom of these élite bands, embodying their spiritual acquisitions to the greatest degree of perfection, there can or must be certain particular individuals, dominating personalities, who, however, can be the leading spirits that they are only because they express with the greatest energy in their own persons the same life and action that animates their companions.

Thus, in sharp contrast with the great mass of the unenlightened, there is developed the type of half-heroic, half-philosophic heroes or virtuosi. A conception of this sort is hardly conceivable in a time like that of the Veda, or of Homer. True, he who had distinguished himself as a fine bard, or as an expert sacrificer, or as an adept and successful priest and sorcerer, may have had his honors in that age, too. But he was always nothing more than the type of a genus, a prominent expert in the use of the tools of the religious trade which had representatives everywhere. But the men whom we are now looking at are something very different. They were, or so appeared to be, persons who possessed a distinctive stamp of their own; they were sublime pathfinders, pioneers, not to be compared with other mortals, steeped in the powers of a peculiar mystical completeness and perfection.

It is a part of the essential character of such men that they are conceivable to the creed of their followers only in the singular. The name of such a single individual is needed as a rally-cry around which the co-endeavorers can unite; and if such a personage never actually existed, recourse is had to the dim recesses of the mythical past for one of the obscurely grandiose names of that misty world, and around it are concentrated their spiritual possessions in which men find such great bliss and often consolation.

Whilst the personal position of the devotee with reference to his religious belief is thus undergoing modification and becoming a very different one, the matter and content of the belief, too, is at the same time assuming a new aspect.

Those supernatural giants, who were the gods of the older age, now cease to govern the world according to human-like caprices. The government is transferred to powers of another kind, which, although they were well-known ere this, in a primitive form, to the intellect, leave the low, contracted sphere of superstition and advance to the heights of thought, which afford a wider vision:—forces and substances which are put in action by the mechanism of an impersonal necessity, their action being the kernel of the cosmic process itself.

These forces and substances are, of course, very different, indeed, from those which modern learning recognises as the recondite fundamental factors of being and happening. As the products of an analysis, which has still to learn the task of being thorough, they are rather the most prominent and first noticeable of the light and shadow masses of the universe, natural laws and impulses which most frequently press upon his attention. Thus, the physical elements like water and fire, members which exert so much attractive force upon the intellect in the youthful period of the human mind, the great impulses of love and hatred, the fluctuation of happening (becoming) and being with its immutable calm. Substances and forces, of which the importance varies with place and people, but which, taken as a whole, have everywhere the same appearance, and therefore belong properly to the same category of reflexions upon the world and its course.

The human soul is the special object to which this

incipient rumination now more and more directs itself. To those ages of spiritual childhood, wholly preoccupied with phenomena, the outer world, follows the period of youth, which gradually becomes introspective, with all the earnestness of youth, all its sense of honor, its heaving bosom panting with the thirst after boundless ideals. The ego is subjected to investigation to see if the secret cannot be found in it for the attainment of those ideals. There is a growing desire to find a clue for the labyrinth of the phenomena of the soul. Efforts are made to dissect its parts or forces; to comprehend the influences mutually exerted by them upon each other; to observe the entrance and cessation of the soul's various functions.

Of foremost importance in these new lines of thought is the idea of the migration of the soul. True, this idea does not suddenly step forth, full-grown and matured, now for the first time. The beginnings of the doctrine appear everywhere to be traceable to the dawn of religion; that the soul of the deceased can make its dwelling-place, temporarily or permanently, in animals, plants, or in other things of every sort, is a belief spread over the whole world among peoples of low civilisation.

It was reserved for the subtler refinement of the age we are now speaking of, however, to impress with the strongest kind of emphasis the additional idea upon this doctrine, of its continuation through endless stretches of futurity, the horror of eternal futility, inexhaustible endurance.

The hitherside of life, which had circumscribed almost all the hopes and desires of the ancients, now appears petty and meaningless, being contrasted with the vast spaces beyond; the terrestrial life becomes a mere place of preparation. Whatever of good one has performed here below, whatever of sin committed, will redound to him over there, perhaps infinitely magnified,—as reward or punishment.

In the literature of an age working on this idea, the type of voyages to the nether world and hell, plays a prominent part: not the mere tales of story-tellers as in the time of the Odyssey, but writings animated with the purpose of picturing vividly to the senses the awfulness and the inexorability of the punishment to be surely expected in the hereafter for even small transgressions. Throughout is dominant an austere, even anxious solicitude, to preserve the personal ego from contamination, even the most trifling, in order to secure for it a completeness and perfection which will impart confidence and hope to it while upon the dark journey of the hereafter. But the chief good, which belongs to such a complete perfection,—the objective point to which those journeys tend,—is the final release from the soul's migration, the exaltation of self over all finite rewards and punishments, the entrance of the soul into the world of things eternal.

It is part of the character of the age here portrayed —that which we have called the spiritual youth of man—that it can recognise as its objective point only an absolute one,—one embracing within itself the absolute perfection. As soon as the intellect grows fond of absorbing itself in the antitheses of the transitory and the eternal, of happening and being, it is unavoidable that the destiny of everything incomplete, imperfected, should appear to be swept along in the stream of the incessant process of becoming and passing away. But in the existence of the perfect, all movement in the sense of change, which necessarily cleaves to the concept of the unattained goal or summit, must have ended; and the dwelling-place of the perfect must lie in some sphere which spreads over and above the inappeasable unrest of the imperfect.

But who is it that may attain to this highest goal? The answer might be and was given: "He who had been purified by special consecrations, by the observance of special mysterious regulations, and even by the precepts of sorcery." But in this age, everything necessarily led to a new turn of belief. Mention has been made of how, in those contracted circles where the thoughts just laid down were cultivated, the thinker's self-appreciation and seriousness induced a growing consciousness of his differentiation from and superiority to those who were without the pale, the thoughtless, the blind. That world of eternal things is intelligible only to the thinker. And the thinker alone, therefore, may participate therein. True, the motive, dating from a far remoter time, which was allowed to the good man,—even the commonplace member of society, so long as he is good,—that of the hope of reward in the hereafter, has not lost all of its old effectiveness. But it is subordinate to the more powerful motive, that the chief and incomparable salvation in a world, of which but the few have knowledge, can accrue, not to the poor in spirit, but only to those elect few, the thinkers, whose whole life is directed to the one pursuit of shaking off terrestrial imperfections, and of thus achieving a citizenship in the empire of things eternal.

There is necessarily much of the local color wanting to our portrayel of these views,—much of all the concrete reality. For the purpose has been to trace the general outline of a particular stage of religious evolution common alike to India and Greece. This general abstract assumed concrete shape in India in Buddhism and its kindred forms; in Greece in a movement first manifest under the cloak of the ancient mysteries, presently struggling again and again toward precision and clearness of thought, as the reflective mind strives to tear the veils which obstruct its vision, only to fall back as often into the former twilight of mysteries again,—all the forms of this movement, however, breathing forth the same spirit, the wishing one's self out of this transitory world into the eternal world.*

Here, prominently, the mysteries of Orpheus present themselves to notice: that mysterious doctrine and cult of sects concentrating about the much-fabled name of the bard of Thrace. Dating, as it appears, from the sixth century before Christ, and cultivated at Athens, and many other places, especially in the Greek colonies of Lower Italy, this doctrine and cult sought to prepare its devotees, as "The Pure," for the future glory by ceremonies of consecration, sacred teaching, and the holy orders of the "Orphean Life." Our knowledge of the peculiar ideas of this cult is very limited. But whoever approaches the little which has been preserved, with the dogmas and the poetry of the Indian mendicant monks in mind, will often be surprised, at coming upon what seems a bit of Buddhism in the midst of Greek civilisation.

Alongside of the Orphean mysteries, and closely related to them, stands the sect of Pythagoreans, established by and named after a man whose powerful,

* The chief features of this movement have lately been portrayed with as much sage penetration, as fine restoration of the sentiment, by E. Rohde, *Psyche* (1893), p. 395 ff. At many points, what here follows is an acceptance of his views.

deeply forceful personality shines through the mist of a meagre legendary tradition with astonishing clearness. Whilst the best-known characteristic of the Pythagorean speculations is the attempt to discover in numbers the most secret and essential kernel of all things, yet our attention here is chiefly to be directed to the efforts of these closely confederated companions to liberate the soul of its imprisonment (for as such they looked upon corporeal existence), and from the bonds of the soul's migration.

We cannot attempt here to follow the current of these religious-philosophical speculations in the Greece of the sixth and fifth centuries B. C., through all its various ramifications. It is, however, to be mentioned that the influence of the Orphean and Pythagorean ideas continues, clearly recognisable, up to the very acme of all Greek thought, up to Plato's time. Plato's conceptions as to the chief aims of human existence stand in closest contact with those of his mystic predecessors. True, it is, with a strength of which the latter fall far short, that his intellect attempts to break the shackles of creed and imagination, and to gain the conquest of a complete scientific certainty. But quickly enough—soonest of all in the problems of the human soul and its future destiny—he, too, finds that he has gotten to the boundary-lines of those regions, the entrance to which is barred to even the philosopher's cognition and proof.

It is Plato's fashion not to stop for such a reason. When the dialectician halts, the poet begins to speak: and in pictures of profound beauty, the poesy of Plato unrolls its grand views of the hereafter, the subterranean realm of the shades, and the realm of light and eternal ideas. He is accustomed to fortify himself by an appeal to what he has heard "from men and women who are wise in things divine"; what Pindar and many other of the poets, "such of them as are inspired," have uttered; but it is especially the Orpheans from whose dark wisdom he loves on such occasions to draw half-mantled and half-revealed matter, images from the same realm, intermediate between thought and invention, in the twilight of which the creations of Buddhism, too, have their being.

We shall next throw a glance at the chief features of both the Indian and the Greek chains of thought, in which embodiments of the type just described in the history of religion may be recognised. The close relationship between the two sets of ideas will be confirmed throughout.

II.

In both Greece and India, societies of devotees were formed. They gave themselves a name which served to remind them of their real or supposed founder, from Orpheus or Pythagoras, just as the "monk-disciples of the son of the Shâkya" did. In close communion with each other, and separated from the masses without, they strive after a salvation which they hope to attain upon the strength of their own particular doctrine and their own particular intellectual and spiritual discipline.

True,—as one of the more recent historians of these Greek developments has already observed,—the segregation of these sectaries from the world was of a much milder character in Greece than in India, corresponding to the differences in the national characters. Among the Buddhists the religious idea takes possession of the whole life of devotees, with unlimited force and austerity. It destroys their mundane existence, with a logical consistency as thoroughly merciless as ever any idea has destroyed man's enjoyment of temporal life.

In the sacred legend, the royal scion, who afterwards becomes the Buddha, thirsting for the life spiritual, flees at night from his palace, where, recumbent upon a flower-strewn couch, his young wife lies slumbering, a young mother, beside her their first and newly born son whom the father has not yet beheld.

Possibly without any credibility in the ordinary historical sense, this legend nevertheless possesses a complete intrinsic veracity. The Buddhist, being most deeply agitated by his craving for redemption, abandons home and wealth, wife and child: they are bonds chaining him down to earthly life. He wanders from place to place, a homeless beggar.

In Greece, there is greater moderation. True, the communities searching for redemption, in Greece too, consider the present world as a place of uncleanness, of imprisonment; but there is no very great seriousness in their efforts to escape from this thraldom. Outwardly they continue to observe the duties and enjoy the pleasures of every-day life, and are satisfied with the practice of securing inwardly a release from the limitations of such a life by the secret power of the mystic doctrine and the mystic cult.

Whatever the peculiarities of the different sets of ideas evolved by these pious communities, the one feature is common to them all: this world appears to all of them as a gloomy domain of dissension and suffering. The symbolism of the Orpheans has it that Dionysus, the divinity, is torn to pieces by Titans:

the blessed unity of all Being undergoes the evil fate of disintegration.

Another Greek conception, of the sixth century B. C., discerns in the material existence of things a guilt; all heavens and all worlds, issuing from unity and infinity, having become guilty of wrong, must pay the penalty and do penance therefor, resolving themselves again into the components from which they originally came into being.

One noticeable trait is introduced into the appraisal of this existence by speculations which are traceable first of all to the great obscure Ephesian, Heraclitus. "All things are in flux,"—all being is a continuous change, self-mutation. "Into the same stream we step and yet do not step; we are and are not." This restless flux of becoming and passing away again is also characteristic of the human soul, which essentially is identical with the least corporeal of the elements, fire. As the existence of flame is a continuing death and re-generation, so the soul lives in the ceaseless production and passing away, in the ceaseless ebbing and flowing of its elements. Its apparently undisturbed continuity of identity is a deception.

True, Heraclitus himself, buoyant and active by nature, did not tint this doctrine with the gloomy color of lamentation that human destiny was therefore all aimless and made up of suffering. But to thinkers, who were inclined to look upon the continuity and constancy of a supreme eternal being as the sole satisfactory reply to their inquiries regarding the end of human life, this philosophical abstraction concerning the nature of material existence was identical with despair in its utter and hopeless emptiness. Thus, to Plato, this is a world of immaterial seeming. Verity and complete satisfaction are obtainable aloft only, in the flights beyond, where are the eternal ideas; thither the soul, fallen from its bright estate, home-sick, yearns ardently to return.

Now contrast with these Greek thoughts their counterparts in India. In the age when the way for Buddhism was being prepared, thought moves exactly in the same lines as it did with Plato, being a contrast of that which is and persists, and that which is transitory. On the one hand, the soul of the universe, the great One, ever untouched by pain; on the other hand, the world of phenomena, the realm of hunger and thirst, of care and perplexity, of old age and death. And, like Heraclitus, Buddhism too sees in this latter world a continuous flux of becoming and passing away, a never-ending concatenation of causes and effects,—the latter in their turn also becoming causes which continue to produce new effects, and so on to infinity. Peace there is alone in the world of "the unborn, of that which has not yet come into being, has not yet been made, has not yet assumed form," in the realm of the Nirvâna.

An early Buddhistic dialogue compares life to a tree, the root of which is perishable and mutable, as are also its trunk, and branches, and leaves: who can believe that the shadow of such a tree will always remain the same and escape the fate of change? "But the unstable—is it suffering or joy?" asks Buddha of his disciples. And they answer: "Suffering, master!" Or, in the words of a stanza, oft repeated:

> "All shape assumed inconstant is, unstable,
> All subject to the fate of birth and death.
> It comes to pass, and soon it vanishes.
> Blessed rest, when th' space of birth and death is done!"

Moreover, we find here exactly the same application of the aforementioned fundamental philosophical views that we do in Heraclitus. In both cases they are applied to the soul and its life. "Disciples!" says Buddha, "That which is called soul, or spirit, or reason, is ever changing and becoming something else, —ceaselessly, day and night, constantly going through the process of becoming and of ceasing to be."

A dialogue of a later time, very remarkable in a historical regard, reproducing throughout the early Buddhistic views, treats of these thoughts in greater detail. It is the conversation of a holy man with King Milinda (the Greek Prince Menander, well-known from coins), who, it seems likely, ruled over the Northwest of India about 100 B. C. Strongly reminding one of Heraclitus, it compares life, personality, to a flame. "When, O great King, a man lights a candle, will not the candle burn through the night?"—"Yes, sire! it will burn through the night."—"How, then? O great King! Is the flame during the first watch of the night the same that it is in the second watch?"—"No, sire! . . . but the light burned the whole night, adhering to the same matter."—"So, also, O great King, the chain of the elements of things is joined together. One element is always coming into being, another is always ceasing and passing away. Without beginning, without end, the chain continues to be joined together."

The identity of the Greek and Indian ideas concerning the nature and destinies of the human soul extends still further. What are the effects upon those ideas of this all-dominant, pain-bringing law which subjects everything to the fate of coming into being only to pass away again? Both the Greek thinkers and the Buddhists alike answer this question by postulating the doctrine of the migration of the soul. Death is followed by a new birth—not necessarily in human form, both the divine and the animal are deemed possible; this re-birth is followed again by death, and this by re-birth: so that the one life is merely an infinitesimal link in a vast chain of lives, to be bound up in which is a great misfortune.

The Orpheans symbolise the migration of the soul by means of a circle or wheel. They speak of the wheel of fate and of birth; the final end of existence seems to them to be

"To release one's self from the circle and breathe anew, freed from distress."

In the inscription of a small gold plate taken from a tomb near the ancient Sybaris, the soul of the buried person, an Orphean, for whom the claim of final release from the migration of the soul is made, exclaims:

"At last I have flown from the circle of ill, the toil-laden ring."

Imagine the rhythm of these hexameters turned into the irregular movement of the Indian *Sloka*-metre, and one might imagine himself in the very midst of the Buddhistic poetry. A Buddhist proverb says:

"Long to the watcher is the night,
To the weary wand'rer long the road,
To him, who will not see truth's light,
Long is the torment of his chain of births."

And another expression, which is put into the mouth of Buddha, at the point when—his trials and struggles over—he has achieved the knowledge of salvation. He is triumphing in the fact that he has penetrated the designs of the wicked foe, those evil powers ruling terrestrial things, who unremittingly are ever reconstructing the corporeal house, the body, and whom he has succeeded in putting away from himself:

> "In vain the endless road
> Of rebirth I have wandered,
> In vain have sought life's builder,
> An ill is this fate of birth.
>
> House-builder! found you are!
> You'll build no more the house.
> Your timbers are all broken,
> Destroyed the house's spires.
> The heart—escaped from earth—
> Has compassed the aim of its search."

And in the same way that the Orpheans symbolise the continuous existence of the migrating soul by means of a circle or wheel, so too the Buddhists speak of the "wheel of lives." Buddhistic pictures usually portray this wheel of existence in such manner that a stage of existence is symbolically shown between every pair of spokes, as the human kingdom, the animal kingdom, heaven, hell; beside the wheel is the form of Buddha, who, as one redeemed, stands without the revolution of existences.

In the dialogue above cited, King Milinda asks the holy man for a parable which shall give a notion of the interminable, beginningless migration of the soul. Thereupon the holy man draws a circle on the ground and asks: "Has this circle any end, great King?"—"It has not, sire!"—That is the same as the circle made by the course of births," the holy man teaches him. "Is there then any end to its succession?"—"There is not, sire!"

And as the Orphean doctrine had it that he who was redeemed "had flown from the circle," so an early Buddhistic proverb says:

"The swan soars through the sun's ethereal pathways;
The sorcerer flies through all the realms of space:
So, sages, rich in wisdom, flee this world,
The prince of death and all his powers o'erwhelming."

One brief glance more at a few of the particular traits of the doctrine of the migration of the soul, common to both India and Greece. It will be plainly seen that the fundamental similitude of ideas has had the effect of making the aspect of even the minuter details in the two religions similar.

One characteristic, very prominent among both peoples, is the very natural connexion of the doctrine of the soul's migration with the idea of moral retribution. The good and the evil which man has wrought in this life will in turn be done to him in another life, meted out to him in the blessedness of heavenly, or in the pain of infernal, worlds.

Naturally, at this point, the popular imagination—widely removed from the colorless abstractions of reflective thought—begins to play a part. Poetry drew all kinds of pictures of the horrors of the infernal world. There was a "voyage to the lower world" in poetry among the Orpheans, and another of the same name among the Pythagoreans; the Buddhistic literature is fairly overrun with innumerable, moral-pointing descriptions of the descents of holy men into the infernal regions and of the horrors there observed by them.*

Opposed to these terrors are the heavenly ecstasies. And here a characteristic appears which is emphasised strongly by the Buddhists, but visible only sporadically in Greece, although entirely the same there.

* We may refer here to the fine description which L. Scherman (*Materials for a History of the Indian Literature of Visions*, 1892) has given of these phantasies.

Empedocles denies immortality to the gods; their longevity is great, but they are not eternal. The divinities of the Veda have in the same way ceased to be immortal to the Buddhists. Possessed of a length of life reaching beyond the grasp of all human standards of measurement, they are, nevertheless, along with others, knit into the chain of the migration of souls; and the human being who has lived a blameless life, dare hope to be born again as a god. No more lively illustration can be found in all the history of religion than this fate of the ancient gods, how an idea—having lost its original import, its own proper life—yet maintains its existence into a later age and is then by the latter animated with a new import, corresponding to the altered views of things.

As still another common Indo-Grecian characteristic of the doctrine of the migration of the soul may be mentioned, that, among both peoples, there were certain especially inspired men, who could, so it was held of them, recall the various earlier embodiments which they themselves and others had passed through. Pythagoras, of whom it was sung that

> "When he with might compelled to the fullest the powers of mind,
> Easily could he th'adventures o'erscan of every existence,
> Through ten, yea, through the vista of twenty past, long human life-spans,"

is said to have related experiences and adventures from his earlier lives. Empedocles said:

> "Thus have I been in former existence a youth, and a maiden,
> So, too, a shrub, and an eagle, a poor mute fish in the ocean."

Exactly so, only exaggerating the marvellous into the boundlessly wonderful, the Buddhistic religion tells how in that holy night in which he first beholds the true knowledge of salvation, as in a vision, the whole picture of his previous forms of existence, through hundreds of thousands of births, passes in review before the soul of Buddha. Tales, recording adventures of the most variegated colors from these past existences of Buddha himself, of his disciples and enemies, accompanied with lessons and applications of every sort, are among the most cherished elements of popular Buddhistic literature. Hundreds of re-births are recounted of Buddha, now as a king, again as a devout hermit, or as a courtier, or as a god, or as a lion, an ape, a fish. And it is well known how inestimable is the value of these stories and fables to the folk-lore studies of our own time—seeing that the motive of them frequently reappears, scattered over the whole earth.

III.

Opposed to the realm of the migration of the soul with all its sufferings, there is, for Greek and Indian thinkers alike, a world of freedom, of the complete cessation of all suffering. Whilst the youthful human mind of the early ages perceived in power and victory, in wealth and long life, the chief joys of life, the supreme end of life is now salvation from the misery of becoming and passing away, rest in the calm glory of eternity.

Among the Greeks, as we have seen, the Orpheans speak of "releasing one's self from the circle," and of "taking flight from the circle." Plato pictures the soul as being rescued from its wanderings and entering into "the community of the divine, the pure, the true to itself." At one time, it is the negative form which this ideal assumes: the release from the suffering of existence. At another, it is the positive form:

perfect, unchanging blessedness. A certain reserve was for the most part observed toward the temptation to make the description of this condition of perfection too concrete and to paint it in high colors: these most beautiful homes of the soul are not easily described, says Plato.

Now this all very closely touches upon Buddhistic ideas. Buddha says to his followers: "As the great ocean, my disciples, is permeated with a *single* flavor, the flavor of the salt; so, too, disciples, is this doctrine and this law permeated with a *single* flavor, the flavor of salvation."

"There is, my disciples, a place where there is neither earth nor water, neither light nor air, neither this world nor that world, neither sun nor moon. I call that, disciples, neither coming nor going nor resting, neither death nor birth. It is without substructure, without progress, without stop. It is the end of suffering."

Sometimes the various turns taken by the Buddhistic texts in which this final aim, Nirvâna, is spoken of, run as if this aim were the termination of all being, or absolute nothing; then again they seem to point to a state of highest perfectiou, surpassing all comprehension and baffling all description. Taken as a whole, the coloring of these thoughts is perceptibly a more negative one than in Greece; and the solution of all too far-reaching questions is declined with greater firmness and readiness. "He who has gained salvation," thus runs a Buddhistic quotation, "surpasses the point where his being can be compassed by the numbers of the corporeal world. He is deep, immeasurable, unfathomable, like the ocean." And at another time, Buddha says to a disciple, who will not suffer a quietus to be imposed upon his questions about the existence of him who has won salvation: "What is not revealed by me, suffer it to remain unrevealed."

As to the ideas concerning the way by which the final highest aim was to be attained—in Greece they rapidly developed in matter and profundity. Early thought still remained essentially under the influence of religious creations which carry the style of remotest antiquity. We know what is the customary practice in the cult of uncivilised peoples, for one who seeks to acquire supernatural power or to ward off evil spirits or death-bringing things of witchcraft. He fasts; he withdraws into solitude; he avoids everything that has any relation with death or similar perils, as food which for some reason or other is considered to be connected with the kingdom of death; by various means he excites within himself ecstatic conditions. This technique of the primitive sorcerer's art, applied to new purposes, maintained itself in Greece as elsewhere with indomitable pertinacity.

It has been justly observed, that a figure like that of Epimenides—an adept master of mystical wisdom, flourishing about 600 B. C., and celebrated throughout all Greece,—bears a number of traits which characterise perfectly the type of the savage medicine-man: fasts and solitude, mystic intercourse with the spirits, long ecstacies, in which he gains his "enthusiastic wisdom." The interdiction of food and—if this ethnological expression be permissible—the observance of taboos of various kinds, among which is very prominent the aversion to all things which in any way remind one of the domain of death,—these are a special vehicle for the spiritual endeavors both of the Orpheans and of the Pythagoreans.

But a new tendency is soon introduced and gains more and more in strength. True continence and purity, so Plato teaches, lie in the purification of the soul from all sensual things, liberation from the passions and desires which "transfix the soul to the body as with a nail" and which compel the soul to endure being reborn in ever new forms of embodiment. The redeemer from these bonds is philosophy, which alone really prepares one for death. Philosophy guides us from the world of constant becoming into that of actual being, into the realm of eternal ideas. The blessed moment of a vision dawns: the curtain before the thinker's eyes sunders, and truth herself shines upon him, in the glory of which immersing itself, the soul is released from the transitory world. In the joy, the bliss of this contemplation, the philosopher, even here below, deems himself in the islands of the blessed. Death, however, forever releases the soul of him, who "has purified himself through philosophy, from corporeality": *his* soul enters into "that akin to his soul, the invisible, the divine, the immortal, the truly wise."

In this last thought, the chain of ideas, which we are now considering, found its culmination. And up to this very point, the Indian ideas follow the Greek ideas in undeviatingly parallel lines.

In India, too, in Buddha's age, the aims of the new spiritual yearning were striven for with the same means from the old cult of sorcery, that we find in Greece—retirement into solitude, exhaustion by severe fastings, and the development of a whole category of ecstatic conditions. For its part, Buddhism rejects fasting as well as every kind of self-torture; but it lays great stress upon the cultivation of those ecstatic meditations, in the exalted calm and quiet of which, afar from the confusing superabundance of form of the material world, it was thought, a presentiment or foretaste might be enjoyed of the final termination of all transitoriness. One of the old Buddhist monkish poets sings:

"When the thundercloud its drum awakes,
Fast the rain sweeps o'er the bird's swift paths,
And in quiet mountain cave the monk
Fosters revery: no joy like that!

"When, along the flowery bank of streams,
Which the forest's motley garland crowns,
He fosters revery, wrapped in blissful calm,
No joy ever can he find like that!"

But that which, before all other things, gives release from earthly suffering is the complete subjection of desire, of "that thirst which but leads from one re-birth to another re-birth,"—the attainment of the pure and highest knowledge.

"Who conquers it—that despicable thirst, which it is difficult to escape in this world—from him all suffering drops like drops of water from the lotus flower."

But this thirst which accompanies earthly existence may be subdued through knowledge,—that knowledge which discovers the misery of the fate of becoming, merely to pass away again, and reveals the cessation thereof in the escape from this world. Since the value or worthlessness of life depends upon the fateful play of great cosmic powers, the endeavor of the devout, the sage, is directed no longer to the object of securing the goods of this world through the friendship of benevolent gods, but to the aim of penetrating the infinite cosmic process, in order that, having mastered it, he may prepare for himself the future place where it is good to be. This last proposition is alike characteristic of the religion of India and of Greece.

Like the ideas of Plato, the doctrine of the Buddhists is that the seeker gains possession of the knowledge of salvation,—after a ceaseless struggle and endeavor continuing through a period of innumerable re-births,—in the sudden inspiration of one incomparable instant of time. He to whom this instant has come has "obtained salvation and beheld it face to face." The Buddhist enlightened one, like the philosopher of Plato, continues to live on earth as a completed being who, in his most fundamental nature, is now no longer an earthly citizen. "The monk who has put away from him lust and desire, and is rich in wisdom, he has even here on earth obtained salvation from death, rest, Nirvâna, the eternal home." And when the end of earthly existence has come, he disappears into those mysterious depths, concerning which Buddha forbade his disciples to inquire whether their meaning is ideal being or absolute nothing.

* * *

The naturalist, studying a cellular structure, will obtain very different views of the same object, according to the direction in which he makes his sections. The direction in which we have contemplated Buddhism made it possible for us to notice the very closest relationship between its fundamental principles and the doctrines of the Orpheans, the Pythagoreans, and Plato. But in conclusion, we must not omit briefly to point out that other lines of consideration would have produced other views and other comparisons of a very different nature.

If we scan the personality of the great Indian promulgator of these ideas, we find at once that Buddha is in all the phenomena of his life, in the manner of his teachings and labors, as widely different from the Greek thinkers as the Oriental character is from the Hellenic. A nimbus of miracles surrounding and glorifying his life, a lofty dignity which overtops all the universe, caps his image in a way impossible to imagine in connexion with the earthly and human figures of Pythagoras and Plato. It is no longer the regions of Greek philosophy, but rather the regions of the Gospels, into which the Buddhistic tradition now seems to conduct us. In fact, some have gone so far—though in my opinion without sufficient reason —as to draw from the striking resemblances of these two fields the conclusion that direct transfers have been made from India to the West. As it was formerly supposed that Pythagoras had drawn his doctrines from Indian sources closely related to Buddhism, so, too, the assumption has found believers—corresponding to the various views taken of Buddhism —that Buddhistic prototypes underlie extensive portions of the Gospels, and that either at Alexandria or at Antioch the intercourse of Christian writers with Buddhistic envoys led to the introduction of a large number of stories, proverbs and parables from Indian literature into that of the New Testament.

It would be possible to carry this identification still further. If along with the person of Buddha and with his doctrine we glance at the third member of the ancient Buddhistic trinity—the ecclesiastical brotherhood or church—we shall be reminded, with sufficient vividness, by the immemorially ancient rules of the Buddhistic order of mendicant monks,—with its deep-rooted aversion to the world, the austerity of its precepts as to poverty and chastity, with its long list of instructions concerning the observance of dignity and reserve, which are manifested after a set fashion in mien and glance, in the manner of eating and drinking, in short, in every gesture,—of Christian monasticism, whether viewed as a whole or in its minutest details.

I think that we may and must be satisfied with the similarity of historical causes at work in the two separate quarters of the world as the explanation for all these resemblances,—a similarity which in my judgment amply accounts for our meeting among civilisations nearer to us in time and place with formations, isolated and scattered, yet closely resembling those which at the height of Indian history, pulsating with Indian life-blood, were united, in Buddhism, into so compact and remarkable a whole.

INDEX.